MASTERING YOUR BALANCE

A Guide To Leading And Living At Your Full Potential

BILL LEIDER & JASON THOMPSON

INDIE BOOKS
INTERNATIONAL®

No part of this publication may be reproduced or distributed in any form or by any means, without the prior permission of the publisher. Requests for permission should be directed to permissions@indiebooksintl.com, or mailed to Permissions, Indie Books International, 2424 Vista Way, Suite 316, Oceanside, CA 92054.

The views and opinions in this book are those of the author at the time of writing this book, and do not reflect the opinions of Indie Books International or its editors.

Neither the publisher nor the author is engaged in rendering legal or other professional services through this book. If expert assistance is required, the services of appropriate professionals should be sought. The publisher and the author shall have neither liability nor responsibility to any person or entity with respect to any loss or damage caused directly or indirectly by the information in this publication.

Mastering Your Balance™ is a pending trademark of Bill Leider.
The Axíes Balanced Organization™ model is a trademark of The Axíes Group.

ISBN-13: 978-1-952233-43-2
Library of Congress Control Number: 2021901644

Designed by Joni McPherson, mcphersongraphics.com

INDIE BOOKS INTERNATIONAL·, INC.
2424 VISTA WAY, SUITE 316
OCEANSIDE, CA 92054
www.indiebooksintl.com

CONTENTS

PREFACE

At their organic core, every organization (including yours) is simply a group of people and some assets, glued together by their purpose and sustained by their *relevance*.

Relevance will determine whether or not your organization remains viable—whether you deserve to exist. In this context, relevance is determined by demonstrating that what you deliver and how you deliver it are needed, wanted, and valued by your customers—and that you can do it profitably. Relevance is the fountain of youth, and it is also a moving landscape. It can be fickle and fleeting. You can be relevant one year and filing bankruptcy the next. That is increasingly true today in our world of rapid, continuous, and disruptive change. The changes we are experiencing are caused by more than just technology; they are a combination of politics, geopolitics, the effects of climate change, societal changes throughout the world, global versus nationalistic ideologies and policies, major movements like #MeToo and Black Lives Matter, a diversifying, multigenerational workforce, increasing income disparity that threatens the future of the middle class, trade policies (such as tariffs), and our education system and its ability to focus on helping to prepare people for meaningful jobs. And if those things were not enough, as I write this, the world is facing the largest pandemic—COVID-19—we've experienced in over one hundred years.

Relevance exists on two levels. The first level ranges from survival to adequate success. It is pretty good, but not exceptional. It's where most companies (and people) live. Those at the top of that level often adjust their perspective and rationalize their achievements as representing excellence. They don't. It just means they have settled for less than their full potential.

The second level of relevance talks to an exceptional level of success that's rare but achievable. It's the arena where true superstars in every field of endeavor play. It requires a constant state of awareness, a high level of the kind of cultural wisdom and strategic adaptability needed to become and remain exceptional, and a commitment to act in ways that continue to sustain that level of relevance.

Understanding the context of what it takes to attain that second level of exceptionalism is what this book is about.

Many of the most popular self-help books frame the ways to improve by using examples of great leaders and achievers. They tell inspiring stories about what those people have accomplished and advise their readers to emulate them. "Do what they do, and you, too, can achieve greatness."

Here's the problem with that framework. You are not them. You didn't have the same developmental experiences they had, the same influences, the same way of feeling, and the same motivations at various pivotal points in their lives. You might not have the same aptitudes or the same strengths and weaknesses. So how in the world are you supposed to emulate them? That is why most self-help books primarily help their authors receive royalties from their sale.

You will be much better served if you learn the elements of brain and behavioral science that can enable you to embrace neuroplasticity (the rewiring of your brain), and become aware of and minimize your confirmation biases (your unconscious, preexisting beliefs that prevent you from accepting new ideas that challenge them). When you do that, you will come to know what kinds of resources you will need (human and capital), how to knock down your self-limiting beliefs about what is possible, and how to acquire the skills to help you succeed beyond your imagination. Then, with the requisite amount of commitment, effort, and persistence, you can become the best possible version of yourself. From that place, you can learn more about why you were put on this planet: how you can make a difference and realize your potential. If you make wise choices, you'll find fulfillment along the way.

I will show you what I believe is the most effective model to help you do all that. It is grounded in *Mastering Your Balance*— which we at Axíes Group define as an aligned state of readiness. The state of your balance and the six elements needed to have a balanced organization (the primary content of this book)—are not a set of skills. Rather, they provide a context for creating a reality and honing your abilities in ways that, if truly mastered, will equip you to achieve levels of success you never imagined— and enjoy continued *relevance*.

The components of balance are not new. You already operate in an organization in which all the elements of balance presently exist in some form, at some level of effectiveness, and with some degree of consciousness. The question is, what are those levels and forms? The answer is vitally important in helping you master your balance and maximize your potential.

An important purpose of this book lies in helping you clearly see how well you are currently functioning with regard to each element of balance, individually and organically (all the elements working together). When you are able to see that, you will come to understand why you are where you are, where your (likely unseen) opportunities lie to maximize your potential, and where to wisely commit your resources to achieve that potential.

You will emerge from reading this book enriched with a newfound sense and sensitivity to the context of what Mastering Your Balance can do to improve your success, what it feels like to go from where you are to an exceptional level of achievement, and for most of you, a compelling sense of commitment to go there.

As you capture that sense of why you are where you are, you'll be able to reflect on how the decisions you made are based in large part on your beliefs about what is possible, what is prudent, what is too risky or too tame, what you are capable of, and what is beyond your abilities.

As you think about the potential within your grasp when you become a more balanced organization, you might also come to realize that *you are not your self-limiting beliefs*. You have them (almost everyone does), but they are not who you are. They don't define you; they don't limit you—unless you let them. The human experience is one of awareness—awareness of all you are exposed to, all you can imagine, all you can achieve— based on your ability, your willingness, and your creativity to gather and harness the resources needed to achieve—not diminished by your self-limiting beliefs.

So, open your mind to experience a new level of awareness and the possibilities that surround you. Let's begin.

CHAPTER 1

Why Balance Matters Now More Than Ever

WHAT IS GREATNESS?

Greatness is a level of being. It is unmarred by changing circumstances. It says: We are always capable of being better today than yesterday, and we can be better tomorrow than we are today. Greatness is sustainable over time; it is not indelibly stamped by a single accomplishment. Greatness is a lifelong endeavor, born of commitment, fueled by passion, traveling along a road dotted with milestones of achievement, while avoiding detours of seductively appealing distractions that promise instant rewards but lead to dead ends of destruction. The milestones are not destinations; they are rest stops to help you rejoice, refuel, and resume your journey. Because the road to greatness has no end.

What makes greatness seem achievable by only a few and seemingly impossible for everyone else? Is greatness preordained? Is it a winning-the-lottery kind of luck? Privilege? Or is it something else, and if so, what is that something?

Perhaps you can achieve greatness by simply working harder and having more perseverance than everyone with whom you compete. Those qualities are needed, but they are not the entire answer. Many people and companies work hard and are still labeled as "average" or "okay but not great." Can greatness be defined by the depth and scope of your subject matter expertise? Only in your own mind. Genius and greatness are two different qualities. Wait, what about a superior business model and a unique value proposition that stand you head and shoulders above everyone else's? Surely that will label you as great. It will certainly take you part of the way, but only if another piece of the greatness puzzle is organically pervasive throughout your organization.

If that mystery piece is working well, it is always present and barely noticed—at least not consciously. It's not part of your product development process, your manufacturing systems, your hiring practices, your sales and marketing plans, or your high-level strategies. Yet it shapes all of those elements and more. Its presence will provide you with the context within which greatness lives. Its absence will assure that, no matter how good you are in all the other areas, greatness will always lie just beyond your reach.

What is that missing piece? It is Mastering Your Balance.

What is balance?

A MASTERING BALANCE PRIMER

Balance is a state of aligned readiness. It is the kind of readiness that enables you to see and seize opportunities quickly and react to crises before they become costly.

Mastering Your Balance is meant to define the actions you must take, the departures from your comfort zones you must make and the skills you must acquire and employ to reach that state of mastery that will define your organization as truly exceptional. Done well, you will experience an endless quest, because exceptionalism is only sustainable if you can continuously adapt to an ever-changing world.

The purpose of this book is to show you how Mastering Your Balance will enable any organization (or individual) to live, learn, and grow more successfully than one that is out of balance—even slightly. An organization, and the people in it, that have mastered balance are able to operate at their full potential. They are higher performers. They adapt well to changes in all manner and magnitude and those that represent both challenges and opportunities. Masterfully balanced organizations are always better able to avoid seductive distractions and remain focused on what matters.

These are the elements of balance:

- **Vision**

- **Values**

- **Values-driven leadership**

- **Culture**

- **Strategy**

- **Greater purpose**

Mastering Your Balance requires continuous, conscious awareness. You must become highly proficient in establishing and living the elements of balance noted above. These elements, taken together, already exist pervasively throughout your company. They provide context for what you do—at every level. If any of the elements are out of alignment, they will cause your organization to perform dysfunctionally. If they are well aligned, they will help enable you to perform at your full potential.

If you think of balance in the context of static equilibrium, please put that belief aside. Instead, embrace the concept of movement and growth in a world of continuous change.

This book will help you develop a deeper understanding of the elements of balance, so you become more consciously aware of how they work together and what can happen when they don't. You will gain a greater sense of the skills and disciplines you will need to achieve and sustain a high level of balance. You will become more adaptive—critically necessary individually, structurally, strategically, and culturally. You will see how your blind spots (we all have them) are hindering your ability to achieve your full potential—and how to uncover and deal with them.

For many years, the media has periodically showered us with stories of the devastating results some iconic organizations had experienced when they suffered from poor management oversight, had inferior leadership, abandoned their integrity to achieve financial goals, or were driven by unbridled greed. Nice list, but it's focused on symptoms. The root causes of their disasters have not been accurately framed. Instead, we have read and heard about people—leaders and followers alike—appropriately found guilty of terrible acts—with no understanding that all these misdeeds are signs of a deeper root cause. *They lost their balance.*

This book will lay out the reasons why, and what they could/ should have done instead. The processes are simple in their essence, and hard as hell to live by. But you will see that had they done those things, the problems could have been foreseen and dealt with before they inflicted untold damages and unimagined costs.

Today, if you were to ask anyone in any of those organizations whether the commitment and work needed to maintain balance would have been worth it, the vast majority of the people would quickly say *yes*. Now, let me introduce you to how Mastering Your Balance works.

HOW MASTERING BALANCE WORKS

The six elements of balance listed above are not new. They've been with us as long as formal organizations have existed. They all exist in every company in some fashion. They might be consciously known throughout the organization and formally documented, with top-of-mind awareness and accountability. Or they exist unconsciously, informally, orally, and implicitly— with inconsistent accountability. Inconsistent accountability is a breeding ground for multiple agendas. Some people apply various elements of balance situationally to pursue fatally seductive short-term objectives. The results of their actions become visible only when the shit of egregious activities hits the fan of public outrage.

Some of you may believe all the elements of balance are working well throughout your organization. They have contributed to your success. Your plans are working well. You are a leader in your industry, outperforming your competitors. Your growth is impressive. Even if that is true, the best companies and the wisest leaders know there is always room for improvement. This book will address some of the nuances that will help guide you to that rare level above excellence.

For the rest of us (the other 99 percent), deep down, you know on some level, you have much to learn about yourself and your organization. Learning those things will help you uncover a wealth of opportunities to raise your own performance bars, begin to transform your organization, and discover what it means to operate at your full potential.

You will harness the power of the six elements of balance based on how and how well you make them seamlessly work together. Just as you don't have to think about remembering to inhale and exhale to breathe, it is possible for you to have the elements of balance ingrained, aligned, and operating at an instinctive level. Developing a deeper understanding of how to go from where you are now to mastery is the journey you are about to take.

To begin, we will first explore how people typically think and what they do that makes them function as an organization from inside the box. You will be given a magic tool you can use to explore how you can achieve seemingly impossible or implausible goals or uncomfortable changes from the status quo. As you read about all the elements of Mastering Your Balance, you will see how to use that tool repeatedly and how you can apply it in your organization.

You will understand why a clear vision can give you a sense of clarity that will serve as your North Star. You will use it to guide your organization toward its long-term legacy. Vision can be your rock of wisdom. You will also see how a lack of a clear vision can infect your organization with a loss of clarity that, in turn, can blur the focus of your strategic goals and take you off course. That same lack of clarity can (and often does) open the doors of your culture to multiple agendas, and the behavioral dysfunctions that accompany them. That, in turn, reduces productivity. And it is all often insidious. It remains unfelt for so long that it becomes your "normal."

You will learn how your stated values, in the absence of measurable accountability for living them, become toothless suggestions. That reality is a fundamental cause of lapses in conduct, performance, and strategic direction that can have consequences ranging from annoying to complete collapse. You will explore how your values shape your culture and how that translates into the quality of your performance, your ability to achieve strategic objectives, your creativity (or the lack thereof), your effectiveness at recruiting and retaining employees—and more.

Values-driven leadership is the art of making everyone in the organization measurably accountable for living your values. This book will show you the bottom-line value of measurable accountability. Values-driven leadership is the antidote to having your values become mere guidelines instead of requirements. You will become more aware of the barriers to creating equal accountability and their cost/performance tradeoffs. You will examine some real-life disasters stemming from nonaccountability that are head-scratchily apparent when seen through the lens of hindsight. And you will learn how you can have the foresight to prevent needless horror stories from occurring.

You will see the many ways in which your culture defines you and determines the kinds of strategies you can achieve (or not)—and why. You will see how your culture (and your values) affect the kinds of talent you can successfully recruit, engage, and retain. You will learn how creative, or not, you can be, what levels of thought diversity are possible. You will realize how those things can affect your growth and your abilities to adapt to change and set and achieve ambitious goals. They all combine to either limit or expand your potential growth and success. You will see how and why you might be holding on to traditional, outmoded cultural practices that have become counter-productive and what you can do about it. Your enlightened view of the breadth and power of your culture just might produce some profoundly mind-expanding revelations.

You will understand strategies in the context of how they align with the other elements of balance (or not) and how that will determine the degree of difficulty and unnecessary costs you will incur, and added time you may need to achieve unaligned objectives, or possibly not being able to achieve certain goals at all. And, you will see how your strategies can be aligned with where you want to take your organization (toward your vision).

Finally, you will see how defining and aligning your greater purpose with the other elements of balance can inspire you, keep your organization relevant (a key to long-term success), and provide a foundation for personal fulfillment—an important contributor to employee longevity, productivity, and morale.

When all that is done, you will tie it all together to paint a picture of what a balanced organization looks like in real life. You'll see the difference between *acceptable* and *exceptional.* And you will get an enlightened picture of where you currently stand. It's the kind of picture the people inside your organization might never show you—even if they see it.

Here's the encouraging reality underpinning all of this. Reaping the benefits is not a question of doing it all or doing nothing. The truth is that no one does it all perfectly. There will always be gaps and temporary lapses. Your path to Mastering Your Balance will be incremental. You can determine the scope and pace. Each insight you gain and apply, each thing you do, each change you make—large or small—will produce measurable gains greater than you ever imagined.

CHAPTER 2

What Would It Take?

W hen I was forty-two years old, I had an epiphany. I realized a question I was asked on the final exam in my college economics class, twenty-two years earlier, could help people envision unimagined possibilities— possibilities that could change outcomes and lives. It was the only question asked on that exam. Here it is.

> *What would it take to grow the world's wheat supply in a flowerpot?*

At the time, I thought the question was just a metaphorical device that required some academic, theoretical answers about the elasticity of supply and demand, alternative choices, various assumptions about production speed, and so on. I could not have been more wrong. I also thought the professor was a whack job. I was wrong about that, too.

Why did it take me twenty-two years to see its value? I couldn't see it because the question, by itself, could create ideas, but those ideas must be plausible and executable to achieve results. The question had to be augmented by a second piece—a mechanism that moves us from thought to plan, to action, and through those actions to results.

Over that twenty-two years, I periodically encountered situations, as an executive and consultant, where seemingly insurmountable obstacles prevented me and the teams I worked with from achieving ambitious goals. Gradually and selectively, at first, I thought about asking *what-would-it-take* questions. When I finally did ask, the results were almost always impressively positive. I improved my skills by asking the right questions at the right times. I also became better at helping others use the approach.

I discovered something else I hadn't seen as a college student. I learned what generations of psychologists, behavioral scientists, and wise people (some of whom are in more than one category) have known for centuries—that *life happens from the inside out*. You dream, create, believe, set goals, plan, decide, act, and achieve. Your future begins from *within you*. When you consciously live that way, you are taking responsibility for the direction and quality of your life. Living from the inside out is the only genuine foundation for being proactive.

Too many people, however, live from the *outside in*—your beliefs and behaviors are conditioned by what others do. You often focus on things you cannot control. You react rather than create. You deal, as best you can, with what comes *at you*, instead of designing what can manifest *from you*. Living from the outside in makes you a perpetual victim; you've given the control of your life to others. It defines you as existing rather than fully living.

So, with twenty-two years of creating my epiphany under my belt, and a few more years of putting into practice what I learned, I realized using the *what-would-it-take* approach had become an instinctive part of who I had become. I finally owned it. Why it took me so long is a question best reserved for a therapist's couch, but that's another discussion. Suffice it to say, the approach has always served me well. It will serve you, too.

When the metaphor of the impossible objective is focused on real-life issues that call for extraordinary measures—whether those issues are about solving problems or exploiting opportunities—prepare to be amazed at the results. It looks like this:

What-would-it-take questions are designed to help you:

- Move your ego out of the process so you can free yourself to explore and create without fear

- Discover and discard your self-limiting beliefs

- Reduce confirmation bias

- Explore new ideas that move you beyond your current reality, taking you to places you might have seen as impossible, impractical, or unreachable

  - Some of those ideas will and should be utterly crazy. It's easier to rein in a wild idea than it is to make a tame idea exciting.

  - Some will be irrelevant.

  - Some will be improbable, but—with some creative approaches and previously untried strategies—just might be doable. Those are your golden nuggets.

WHAT-WOULD-IT-TAKE QUESTIONS IN ACTION

Here are a few real-life summaries I have experienced with company leaders and followers when I encouraged them to ask some *what-would-it-take* questions. I will examine their stories in greater detail later in the book. Their names are omitted for purposes of confidentiality.

A large, premium home appliance company had a vision. It would *revolutionize* the premium home appliance industry. But its new product development cycle required three years—far too long to make it revolutionary. So, its leaders asked, *"What would it take to shorten our new product development time from three years to eighteen months?"* In working with the company over the course of a year, it actually reduced its development time to one year—and realized some additional unforeseen benefits. A major part of its transition required it to change from being a "best efforts" culture to one of making firm commitments—and holding everyone accountable for meeting them. That one change within the product development department became a catalyst for creating a culture of making and keeping commitments throughout the company. A second question was also asked: *"What would it take for us to trust our outside vendors enough with confidential information so we can bring them into the development process early on to help solve manufacturing design problems?"* Successfully addressing just that issue shortened the process by several months. The foundation of that change lay in building mutual trust by first becoming more trustworthy itself. The company had struggled with that unsuccessfully for years.

The consulting division of a large technology company asked, *"What would it take to double our size in one year?"* It asked the question of itself after receiving an edict from its CEO to grow the division by 50 percent in one year. When that edict was received, everyone in the division was already working eighty-hour weeks, senior managers were traveling 75 percent of the time, and morale was low. The division had been growing at an annual rate of 25 percent and was satisfactorily profitable. But the leader of the division knew its opportunities for growth could yield far more than the 50 percent jump the CEO wanted. So, the question was refined: *"What would it take to double our size in one year while reducing hours worked and travel time by 25 percent?"* Subsequently, the division grew by 72 percent. It also achieved its goals regarding hours worked and travel time. It was an eye-opening lesson in adaptability and what could happen when many self-limiting assumptions were unearthed, discarded, and replaced with aggressive and creative strategies to stimulate growth. By the way, the division developed two plans: the first one projected the 50 percent growth demanded by the CEO; the second one, which was actually used, projected 100 percent growth. The CEO only saw the 50 percent version of the plan.

Eighteen individually owned document management/ copier dealers were growing at an annual rate of 5 percent, the same rate as their market was growing. As part of a pilot program supported by their multinational product maker, I helped them ask themselves, *"What would it take to grow our businesses at a rate four times greater than the growth rate of the market?"* They did it by changing some longstanding, traditional cultural habits in their selling process that failed to differentiate them from their competitors. They replaced them with new behaviors that proved profoundly effective. They went from closing 25 percent of their final presentations to a closing rate of 75 percent. And sales grew by 20 percent. It was, in retrospect, shockingly simple. It's a great illustration of what can happen when you allow your deeply entrenched beliefs about people's assumed skills and roles to be creatively challenged.

The IT department of a major motion picture company was hopelessly behind schedule in meeting the needs of the twenty operating divisions it served. It was not for lack of effort. But no matter what was done, the IT group and its internal customers were never on the same page. I asked those twenty divisions this question: If given a choice, would you want to continue to work with your IT department or have your needs served by an outside vendor? All twenty said they would rather use an outside vendor. So, the CTO and her senior managers asked themselves: *"What would it take to dramatically improve the relationship between our department and the twenty internal divisions we serve and have those groups be thrilled with our performance?"* Over the course of one year, the department turned those divisions into highly satisfied customers. Its achievement was dramatic—and required changing its internal culture and learning some new behaviors. The transition was made from *trying* to hit performance targets (and always failing), to *making commitments* to hit realistic targets that addressed everyone's needs (and succeeding). The conduct of its inter-departmental meetings radically changed and produced unimagined improvements in effectiveness. Its cultural change ushered in a new climate of trust—a new climate of collaboration emerged, and its world changed. A year later, when asked the same question about choosing the IT department or an outside vendor, all twenty divisions chose their IT department.

IMAGINE THE IMPOSSIBLE

At the time all the questions were asked, almost everyone in those organizations considered the goals to be unattainable. That brings into play an important dimension in framing the question to yield the most effective results. It is this:

> *To achieve the improbable, you must first imagine the impossible.*

The examples I used above spoke to big challenges and opportunities. But the *what-would-it-take* question is ubiquitous. You can use it to address situations of any size, from the simplest to the most complex. And you can, and should, use it continuously during the process of addressing an issue. Every time you hit a snag during the course of your execution, ask, *"What would it take?"* That continued use is critical to your success.

Given its pervasive usefulness throughout any organization, you should use the *what-would-it-take* question as a fundamental tool to help change and improve all the elements of balance. It will better align the elements collectively and strengthen each one individually.

For example, you can use the question to address issues like:

Suppose your company clings to outmoded cultural norms that limit the range of your hiring practices. You only hire people whose thinking and backgrounds mirror your existing culture and compromise your ability to think outside the box. You could ask: *What would it take to make our company more diverse by hiring people with different backgrounds and ways of thinking, but who still share or can adapt to our values?*

Let's say you need to change your accounting and reporting systems to new software. It requires that your people learn new skills and new procedures. You have valuable, long-term employees who forcefully, or passive-aggressively, resist the change and insist the new systems will make things worse, not better. But you know differently. The new systems will substantially reduce your operating expenses and give you better information. Your people dig in their heels, and the system conversion is going nowhere. You could ask everyone involved: *What would it take for us to embrace the change by being open to making the behavioral and cultural changes needed to make the conversion successful and reap the benefits?*

Imagine you operate a chain of retail stores. You're doing well, but you know your sales associates are not delivering a consistently great brand experience simply because a good number of them do not enthusiastically greet customers quickly enough and with a genuine, welcoming smile that demonstrates respectful recognition. You know it's costing you sales, but it's difficult to connect the numbers to specific employees. You could ask a representative group of your people: *What would it take to turn every sales associate into a great brand ambassador by having everyone in the entire company consistently approach every customer with a warm, welcoming smile and a respectful greeting?*

Each of these questions is simple, basic, and obvious—no magic here. But they will cascade down into the company and generate additional questions that quickly reach granular levels.

Questions about diversity in hiring can, for example, uncover the presence of confirmation bias held by some people responsible for hiring that makes it impossible for candidates with different views to make it past the initial screening process based on appearing to fall short on other criteria. So, what seemed like a shortage of diverse candidates is really something very different.

Resistance to embrace new software by some veteran employees, who use system shortcomings to defend their positions, could easily mean they don't really understand how the change could enhance their skills and make their work more fulfilling. A fresh, interactive approach that better illustrates the benefits to the employees affected might unlock an expensive bottleneck.

Inconsistencies in the way sales associates greet customers might be hiding a number of underlying causes. It's possible your hiring process does not effectively screen out people who simply don't like people. (It happens more than you might think.) Some store managers might be tolerating less-than-desired performance by people who do just enough to meet their minimum goals because the managers don't like to interview and hire new people. Or it could simply be ineffective training of all sales associates.

I could list hundreds more examples, but I think you get the point. As I stated above, each question will elicit a range of approaches, and only a few of them will be adoptable. But those few, well executed, will yield results well above your current expectations. This technique has never failed me. From the most high level to the most day-to-day, gritty barrier, this process works.

You now know about the secret tool. What took me twenty-two years to learn is now yours. You can put it to work immediately. We can now turn our attention to examining each of the six elements of balance. In the process, you'll get a stronger sense of how *what-would-it-take* questions can help you accelerate your performance and raise your potential to achieve greater bottom-line results.

CHAPTER 3

Envision Your Vision

VISION: *A thought, concept, or object formed by the imagination; a future reality, not yet manifest.*

Your vision should serve as a target for the direction and objectives of your strategies and the focus of your culture. It should be a source of inspiration and navigation. It is your North Star—and more.

Your vision also forms part of the platform on which you function at ground level. It can influence how your culture operates and navigates as you move over time. You experience the tangible influence and effects of your vision through a variety of behaviors and outcomes. Yet few people make a conscious connection to the scientific explanations that describe how and why specific behaviors occur. Those behaviors emerge and operate in what is commonly known as a complex adaptive system. The term itself, while it may sound a bit esoteric, is simply a title used to explain the scientific foundation and the ways and reasons for how the characteristics work as they do. The bodies of science involved in all this are biology, behavioral science, and neuroscience.

Exactly how are the operating characteristics of a complex adaptive system affected by your vision? Let me explain. The characteristics of complex adaptive systems exist in every situation:

- That involves people

- When the organization must deal with many moving parts (complexity)

- When continuous change (quickly or slowly) occurs in predictable and unpredictable ways

- When the people in the organization must assess, interpret, and react to those changes (adaptability) in an organized way so as to keep moving toward your goals.

So your vision becomes one of the guardrails of conduct that help clarify the focus and direction your actions will reflect—if it is known and consciously embraced by everyone. When I say actions, I mean the behaviors of people in your organization in response to how they assess the situations and conditions they encounter in their day-to-day activities. If, however, your vision (and your values as well) are somehow ignored, the behaviors you experience will also reflect that abandonment.

WHEN YOU ABANDON YOUR VISION

Here is an example of vision abandonment. Wells Fargo's vision is:

> *We want to satisfy our customers' financial needs and help them succeed financially. This unites*

us around a simple premise. Customers can be better served when they have a relationship with a trusted provider that knows them well, provides reliable guidance, and can serve their full range of financial needs.

For whatever reasons, conditions on the ground in its retail division caused people to assess their situation and behave in ways that completely contradicted this vision. What drove those assessments and how could the characteristics of a complex adaptive system explain this ultimately self-destructive behavior?

Here is one possible explanation. It began at the senior leadership in the retail division. They seemingly disregarded the bank's vision when they set overly ambitious objectives for a group of over 5,000 line employees charged with generating additional revenue by cross-selling new accounts and credit cards to existing customers. It appears most of those employees were either untrained or undertrained. They could not deliver at the pace and in the volume demanded by leadership. No additional training was made available. The goals were not modified to align with the skill levels of the employees. Instead, the consequences of not achieving the goals were punitive, not remedial.

The employees assessed the situation, and without formal orders to do so, created new accounts without notifying their customers. It was blatantly fraudulent. No, they all didn't do it simultaneously. A few began. They hit their numbers. Their supervisors either did not know they did it fraudulently or knew and did not care. When the first wave of employees succeeded in hitting their goals and went unpunished, more followed. The combination of continued pressure from above to perform, and the innate desire to gain acceptance from their peers and keep their jobs, drove the rest to adopt the new ways. It was all done in the spirit of achieving the stated objectives handed down by senior leaders.

To the people on the ground, however, the scenario plays out to a different narrative. No one who is going through that kind of situation looks at what is happening to them through scientific, clinical eyes. They don't take a breath and think, *Oh wow. I'm experiencing a change in circumstances. My assessment of those changes tells me that I must adapt my behavior consistent with the ways in which people operate in a complex adaptive system.*

What happens in real life looks more like, *Holy shit. There's no way I can hit these goals. My boss is a total asshole. But wait. They told me if I don't make my numbers, I'm toast. If that happens, I will have about two weeks of severance pay and the $6 in my savings account. And no immediate job prospects. I'm gonna talk to the other people in my group. We're all in this mess together—I think. And yeah, all that talk and those fancy wall posters about our vision and our values—it's all crap. My trust in leadership has just left the building.*

The line employees overtly and intuitively collaborate. They learn they are indeed all experiencing the same feelings and the same assessment of their predicament. They pretty much collectively agree that they must game the system—cheat and commit fraud—or be tossed out. So, one by one, a daring few at first, followed by a growing wave of followers, start opening new accounts and issuing credit cards to existing customers without notifying them or getting their approval.

And they get away with it. OMG. After a month or two of seeming success, two things happen. First, they hit their numbers. No one questions how they did it. The intense pressure is off. Second, the angst, the stress, and the sleepless, worry-filled nights begin to dissipate. New habits take hold. Patterns of behavior, initially seen as reprehensible, are now accepted as the new normal. The employees can breathe. For years, life seems okay. Until one life-altering day, it isn't.

This is but one example of how the characteristics of a complex adaptive system work in the world. I used an example that produced an unwanted result because it more clearly illustrates both the mechanics and the power of those forces.

YOUR VISION AS A STRUCTURAL CORNERSTONE

Think about how this would apply in your organization. When the clarity of your vision is fuzzy, or you don't keep it top-of-mind among all the people in your organization, or you don't even have a vision, you will have created room for a variety of interpretations about the focus of your strategic goals—mostly in unintended directions. That, in turn, will cause people to adapt their behavior to any changes that occur as a result. This is true whether the cause of the change is internal and within your control or external and you cannot control when and how it occurs. On the flip side, when your vision is clear, and your values inspire the behaviors that align with it, they become guardrails that better direct the behavioral flow of your culture, so your people become and remain aligned with where you want to go.

I will go into more detail about how this plays out in your organization in the chapter about culture. That is the area where the tangible effects of your vision show themselves in sometimes dramatic ways through the actions and adaptive capabilities of your people. If you can see peoples' adaptations to changes through the lens of a complex adaptive system, you will have broadened and deepened your understanding of why your cultural behaviors are what they are and what you can most effectively do to prevent problems from arising and affect change when change is called for.

For now, however, it is most important for you to embrace the fact that your vision is both your North Star and a structural cornerstone of your everyday actions—provided you craft it with clarity and keep it alive in everyone's consciousness. If you only create a vision because you think it's politically correct, or you feel the need for an impressive wall plaque in your lobby—none of this will make sense.

With that contextual understanding in place, let's examine how visions are typically developed and what similarities they express.

Visions typically fall into one of three categories:

- Aspiring to become a better version of your current self

- Aspiring to grow beyond your current state of being, embracing a singular or continuous reimagining and reinvention of your current business

- Some combination of the first two

Some business leaders are first and foremost problem solvers. Some tend to be conceptually reactive rather than proactive. They are pragmatic, *"I'll believe it when I see it"* people. Some go so far as to believe that having a vision is pointless. If you are in the latter group, I hope this chapter will help you revisit that position.

Business leaders who are more creative and open-minded about how they view their future tend to be "*I'll see it when I believe it*" people. They are conceptualists. For them, creating an imaginative vision seems natural.

But whichever you are, visions are valuable in any organization. Believing in an as-yet-unseen reality does not mean you disconnect from the nuts and bolts of the present. On the contrary, having a North Star can move you toward a fulfilling future more directly, effectively, and profitably. Especially if you have ambitious growth plans.

Your vision bridges the time gap between your current reality and idealized future. It clarifies the path you intend to take to create your legacy. Using it to guide you continuously helps you avoid seductive distractions and stay on your chosen path.

Pragmatic visions that essentially say, *"Let's just stay the course. We want to keep getting better at what we already do"* typically convey a sense of stability. They tend to be clear, and they contemplate few, if any, cultural changes in behavior. If this describes you and your organization, you must take special care to hire and retain people who are motivated by doing and getting progressively better at variations of the same things for their entire careers.

Many pragmatic people don't spend the time or invest the effort to see the connection between the intangible concept of a future reality and their measurable and executable plans to increase sales, earnings, and shareholder wealth. The two, they argue, are vastly different and irreconcilable. All thinking, they believe, must be visibly tied to either solving a problem or exploiting an opportunity. Quantifiably unmeasurable goals have no meaning.

They are wrong.

On the conceptual side, it takes courage to tell the world about your vision. You are stepping out of the comfort of the known. You are giving voice to an idea, a concept, a place only you can see. It's a way of being you haven't yet achieved. If your vision is big, almost everyone will think you're nuts—at first. You are the Wright Brothers believing humans can fly. John F. Kennedy telling America his vision is that people will travel in outer space. Steve Jobs imagining a device currently used just to send and receive telephone calls will transform the world and become the dominant control center used to connect, educate, drive commerce, and entertain the planet in unheard-of ways.

When it's just you out there, you are disconnected from leadership, because for the moment, you have no followers. But relax. As soon as one other person aligns with your vision, you are once again a leader.

I've never seen a line item labeled "progress toward achieving our vision" appear on any kind of performance report in any company I've led, worked with, or read about. It's difficult to stay engaged with something that lives in our thoughts but is rarely discussed in day-to-day affairs. It's present yet invisible, powerful yet quiet, designed to provide steady guidance but all too often ignored.

There is a secret to crafting an effective vision, one that will become a true guide to your direction and will keep you accountable for adhering to your vision's message. Your vision must make the conceptual practical. To do that, you must make your strategic goals visibly connected to progress toward your vision. You must find ways to communicate that information. And you must require people to consider that connection— between the practical acts of doing and the future reality described in your vision—when formulating and executing strategies. You must be able to connect the disparate dots of the peripheral and unintended consequences of your actions to either measurable progress toward or detours that lead away from your vision. Easier said than done, but essential. Great leaders work hard to master that skill.

There is a wealth of material written on the profound importance of having a vision, and of its essential role in helping guide people and organizations to ascend to seemingly impossible heights.

Winston Churchill said: *"The empires of the future are empires of the mind."*

Michelangelo stated: *"The greater danger for most of us lies not in setting our aim too high and falling short; but in setting our aim too low, and achieving our mark."*

Most of what has been written talks to the conceptual side, and the value of vision as a source of inspiration, focus, and commitment. It creates a context for commitment as it answers the question: commitment to what?

YOUR VISION AND PRACTICALITY

But what about the practical aspects regarding vision in business? Some say practicality breeds limitations as to the scope and grandness of a vision. They're right, yet those limitations might be necessary if your vision has a chance of being used for all the good things it can help you achieve. Here are some of those major limitations:

Public companies must bow to the unceasing demand by shareholders and the financial community to increase shareholder wealth. That demand creates the kind of stress that leads leaders to bend (or break) the rules; abandon wiser, long-term strategies; and pursue short-term opportunities that address the perceived need to cater to the self-interest of shareholders. It's difficult to imagine a future reality built on achieving long-term objectives when your own future depends on meeting the immediate earnings goals established by ninety-day revenue and earnings forecasts influenced and sometimes entirely established by Wall Street analysts.

Many privately held companies (typically small and midsized businesses) are owned and led by people whose picture of the future does not extend past their own working lives. Their visions are more personal. They envision a company that can provide for their families and achieve their goal of a comfortable retirement. What happens after that is not their concern. If you are one of those people or work for one, there is no shame in that. But it does inhibit the size of your dreams and the scope of your imagination. It has been said the best way to increase the fair market value of a business is to lead and run it as if it were going to remain viable for the next one hundred years. A vision that extends beyond the working life of the owner has consistently been shown to create a greater fair market value of the business, no matter when the owner chooses (or is forced) to sell the company.

Fear—the proverbial elephant in the room—always present but rarely acknowledged. Fear is a many-headed monster. It is a master of disguise. It can look like rational justification, steering a steady course, fueled by shareholder expectations while cleverly hiding an inability to embrace disruptive change and ill-prepared to develop a continuously adaptive culture. Fear can make your engine run fast—with your gear stuck in idle. Fear will also manifest as a rejection of anything that cannot be measured in quantitative terms and presented on a performance report. "We don't believe in that soft and fuzzy stuff" is one way to dismiss the idea that a vision should be entertained at all. But there's nothing soft and fuzzy about a company whose market value is substantially increasing every year.

Where does all of this take us? What, in a real-world sense, can connect the conceptual—that implausible dream perched beyond the horizon of the present—to the rigors of execution needed to focus and perform in ways that actually achieve something worthy of being called your vision?

It begins with you coming from a place of authenticity. Without authenticity, your vision is worthless. You will ultimately be seen as a phony, disrespected as a true leader. Authenticity is more potent than boldness, more inspiring than creativity, and more likely to succeed than intelligence. Authenticity begets trust. Without trust, true commitment is impossible. Without commitment, the greatest dreams will not pass the test of overcoming adversity.

From that place of authenticity, you must create *alignment*. Your vision must align with your values and your culture and vice versa. Without that seamless connection, your ability to brilliantly execute is all but impossible. Your vision descends from pursuable dream to delusional fantasy.

Your strategies must align with and move you toward your vision. You cannot allow yourself to be seduced by the temptation of immediate and inordinate gain when it comes at the price of allocating your finite resources away from your true purpose—your vision—and squanders your opportunity to build the future you want.

What I've discussed above relates to companies with bold, creative visions. Now let's look at those with more pragmatic visions: becoming better versions of what they already are.

PRAGMATIC VISIONS

Some industries are designed for steady, conservative growth along a predictable road. Risk is the enemy of wisdom. The banking industry is a good example, although many banks and bankers saw it differently (and still do). They created instruments like derivatives and interest rate swaps, conceived as hedges against risk—except when markets behaved in unforeseen ways and human behavior defied conventional logic. Too many bankers (and others in the financial industry) in the years leading up to 2008, treated depositors' money as their own piggy banks. They went nuts with risky bets—partly to profit their banks, and partly with a generous portion allocated for personal gain.

They lost sight of their stated visions and the values (and strategies) that aligned with them. If those visions had remained in their consciousness, if they weren't seduced by the allure of once-in-a-lifetime financial gains from what, in hindsight, were boneheaded gambles, where would we be today? I know I'm vastly oversimplifying the root causes of the financial collapse of 2008. My point, however, is that banks played a significant role. And one of the reasons was, perhaps, that they lost sight of their visions—or maybe they just decided their visions became irrelevant when held up to the otherworldly financial opportunities in front of them.

Here's an example. Let me once again reference Wells Fargo. Its vision, again, is this:

> *We want to satisfy our customers' financial needs and help them succeed financially. This unites us around a simple premise. Customers can be better served when they have a relationship with a trusted provider that knows them well, provides reliable guidance, and can serve their full range of financial needs.*

It suggests that Wells Fargo's vision is to continue to do better at what it already does. It is not a dream. It's more of a strategic initiative. There are few, if any, forks in the road. Just keep on keepin' on. From time to time, someone might develop a new product or service. But for the most part, their tomorrows will look pretty much the same as their todays. They have refined the definition of vision as a future reality not yet manifest to mean *that we will continue to be an ever-improving version of who we are for a very long time. Our future will be an enhanced version of the present.*

As we already discussed in a different context, recently uncovered events that took place over the last ten or so years suggest the Wells Fargo team didn't look at its vision very often. It didn't seem to provide much, if any, guidance. The same can be said for its values, and I'll talk more about that in the chapter on Values. My point is, a vision that sounded right for the kind of business it's in (or is supposed to be in) was laid out. It wasn't glamorous. Or daring. Or life-changing. But it was probably what a bank should be about.

Instead, some of Wells Fargo's executive leaders took the bank down a path of mind-bending self-destruction, costing billions of dollars and curtailing their growth for years to come. The bottom line is this: Wells Fargo did not get into trouble because it had a faulty vision; it got into trouble because it had a good vision—and trashed it.

Here's an important lesson from its experience: If you're going to take the time to create and articulate a vision, make it one you are committed to following. Make it one that helps you curb your natural desires to stray off course when a seemingly irresistible opportunity pops up. And make it one that is worded and understood in ways that allow you to hold people accountable for staying on course.

That may sound preachy. But our business highways are littered with the wreckage of once-good companies, led by smart people that made good products—until they forgot about all the values and cultural norms that should have emerged from that simple, profound thing we call their vision.

VISIONS AND POSITIVE RESULTS

Here are some examples of companies that are experiencing positive results with their visions:

General Motors has this vision: *To become the world's most valued automotive company.*

This is another company articulating a vision that essentially says, "We want to keep getting better at what we're already doing." By using the words "to become," it's intimating that it is not currently the most valued company. So, it's saying it must do more—it aspires to reach higher levels of quality, performance, and brand experience, but all of it inside the box in which it already operates. That's constrained ambition.

Embodied in this vision, General Motors sees itself progressing without significantly evolving. It currently is and intends to continue to be an automotive company. That may work well. On the other hand, some experts ponder the future of transportation as the improvement and adoption of electric cars (or some other green alternative to fossil fuels) becoming mainstream. They also attempt to project a future in which self-driving vehicles become the overwhelmingly dominant model of transportation. Some others predict most people will no longer own cars; they will simply place a call, then a suitable, self-driving vehicle will appear within minutes, take them to their destination, and drive off.

Experts outside of GM who see this future also see the transformation of cars as electromechanical machines as something much different. They see cars and trucks as computers on wheels, designed for a different ownership and transportation experience while still delivering the transportation, performance, and style elements of traditional vehicles—but better. America's love affair with cars as we know them today will become a nostalgic relic. In that scenario, a lot of credible people see technology companies, not automotive companies, as winners in that race to the future. They reason the creators of today's cars will be too constricted and uncreative in their thinking to compete with the technology people, who are not constrained by yesterday's traditions. The techies will start with a clean sheet of paper and see transportation as something that needs to be radically reimagined, not as evolving from what it used to be.

By virtue of its vision, is General Motors envisioning that race in a way that preordains it losing? Visions spawn cultures that result from attracting people who align with them. Those people will exhibit behavioral norms that influence strategic appetites and directions. Can you see where this is going? A narrow vision, when followed, can lock you into a mindset that embraces incrementally improving on the past but cannot easily adapt to disruptive changes that might define the future.

IKEA has this vision: *To create a better everyday life for the many people.*

To me, this defines IKEA as a lifestyle company. It could take it beyond the furniture, cabinets, and accessories it currently sells. It creates the freedom and space to explore and expand the ways to "create a better everyday life for the many" while still retaining the parts of its company that remain relevant.

Its vision is also different in tone from those of Wells Fargo and General Motors. IKEA's vision looks at its future through the needs and wants of its customers without necessarily connecting future customer needs to its present business. That suggests a revolutionary mindset rather than one that is evolutionary. Big difference.

How might its vision affect the kinds of people it hires? Maybe it doesn't change many of the skill sets it's looking for. But it could change some other behavioral characteristics of those people. IKEA might need to hire people who embrace change as a constant way of life. A person who thinks conceptually versus someone who does well at following instructions and doesn't consider other possibilities would also seem likely. IKEA might want people who see the metaphorical connections between something that seems different and disconnected from what IKEA does, yet might be the source of a golden opportunity if seen through metaphorical eyes.

What kind of culture might exist at IKEA that would be eons different than the culture at a company like General Motors? Why might a person who excelled at General Motors be a bad fit at IKEA, and vice versa?

What kind of strategies might be conceived and executed at IKEA that would be seen as irrelevant, unfocused, and distractive at a company like General Motors?

Southwest Airlines' vision is: *To become the world's most loved, most flown, and most profitable airline.*

Southwest has put its culture at the forefront of execution to move it toward the realization of its vision. It sets the stage for required alignment with the other elements of balance. Southwest put in place three core values that defined how it wants its people/culture to behave to achieve its strategic objectives and move it toward its vision: *a warrior spirit, a servant's heart, and a fun-loving attitude.* I'll go into more detail about those values in the next chapter. The important thing is that they are aligned with its vision. These two elements, when working together, start to become a force multiplier.

As to most loved, Southwest is regularly ranked as a most-favored and reputable airline and as a favorite place to work. In 2017 and 2018, it was ranked highest in customer satisfaction among all low-cost carriers by a J.D. Power satisfaction study. It was ranked eleventh on *Fortune's* list of the world's most admired companies.

As to Southwest's financial returns, it has been profitable for forty-seven consecutive years—an accomplishment few, if any, other airlines have achieved. You can only do that when your flights are full, or close to it, all the time. Over the last few decades, it grew from being a regional carrier to becoming a national one. An investment in Southwest of $10,000 in

1990 would have been worth $540,000 in 2019. Do you see anything intangible in that? Neither do I.

I think the connection between Southwest's vision and the steps it has taken and continues to take to achieve it are obvious. And enviable. And doable.

LEGO's vision is a concept designed to create a picture of what it aspires to be. Here's how its former CEO, Kjeld Kirk Kristiansen, described it in 1988: *"In my vision—in my dream—the LEGO name is associated not only with our products and with the company. And it is not limited within the confines of specific goals and strategies. The LEGO name has become something universal. A concept which can be defined by the words: ideas, exuberance, and values."*

He then burnished it by adding the qualities and characteristics those three words symbolize:

- **Ideas** embraced: creativity, imagination, unlimited discovery, and constructionism

- **Exuberance** embraced: enthusiasm, spontaneity, self-expression, and being unrestrained

- **Values** embraced: quality, caring, development, innovation, and consistency

LEGO's vision includes a profoundly important element. It has made its values an explicit part of its vision. That is genius. Here's why.

Its vision embodies a way of being, of understanding and honoring a particular state of wonder and awe that excites people. Its products must ignite the creative spark in the minds and actions of its audience. It describes the kinds of people who work at and with LEGO, with mindsets that will bring its vision to life. And by including its values in that vision, it is also recognizing and mandating the beliefs and behaviors its people must hold and practice to make all of it real and attainable.

When a vision is taken seriously (and it always should be), you establish the foundation for widespread structural, cultural, behavioral, and strategic decisions, direction, and outcomes. In the absence of vision, it is much more likely you will run a company that will find itself being more reactive. When your course is not set, it's easy to see costly distractions as enticing opportunities. You waste assets, especially human assets. You deprive yourself of the resources you need to examine, choose, and execute the kinds of opportunities that would best serve your long-term interests. And most importantly, without the clarity a vision provides, you lose an important guardrail that helps prevent your people from forming opinions and adopting behaviors that do not reflect where you want to go and how you want to get there. The characteristics of complex adaptive systems kick in and cause some of your people to take unwanted detours. Why would you want to do that to yourself?

In the examples of vision above, there are some useful points to consider.

In the Wells Fargo and General Motors examples, we find visions that want stable, steady, predictable, measurable paths toward their futures. Every constituency can see what the leaders see. No surprises lurking around the corner. A road with few forks. The only predictable hiccups might come in the form of regulatory changes that would alter the product and service offerings and produce either challenges or opportunities. But there is a reasonably long ramp-up period and lots of warning signs along the way. You can also see the effects on results when one company attempts to follow its vision—General Motors— and the other completely ignores it—Wells Fargo.

Looking at IKEA, it has a vision that appears to open doors of possibilities no one can see yet. So, having people who are excited by the opportunities to explore new roads, discover new things, live in an agile culture, embrace the unknown, and perhaps reinvent themselves in the process would seem to define the profile of an IKEA person. Probably not a good fit for a security-minded banker.

Southwest Airlines and LEGO have strong visions made even more tangibly executable because they infused their values into their architecture. By doing that, they created more clarity as to what it will take to move ever closer to achieving their vision. They also helped strengthen the operational alignment between their vision and values. Good move.

How do these examples of predictable patterns align with your beliefs and your approach to defining your vision?

STAYING RELEVANT AND AUTHENTIC

Here's a common thread shared by all of the examples. These visions do not have an end in sight. All of them are about following a path that continues to define them but never to complete them. Having and following that kind of vision will help you stay relevant.

There's another common thread, most visible in the vision of IKEA. While it exists within the context of their respective businesses, it also points to a greater purpose beyond profits and shareholder wealth. That greater purpose is a driving force for making employees enthusiastic about coming to work each day. It stimulates creative attitudes and cultures. It's one more bit of evidence that proves the connection between the elements of balance and actions it continuously takes toward mastering their balance.

Can you see the importance of deeply reflecting on the future you want to create? And having seen that, can you see the inspirational and practical benefits that scream the need for you to create your vision? Can you also see how the absence of doing that can make you an unwitting victim of events and circumstances that will toss you around like a tin roof in a tornado? You might be able to react, but you will never be able to direct. Are you okay with that?

I said it before, but it bears repeating. Your best course is to replace ambiguity with authenticity and clarity. If you have a world-changing vision, unleash it. And if you simply want to become a better version of who you already are, that can be equally effective—as long as that's the truth. I cannot emphasize this enough: authenticity builds trust. Anything less erodes trust. It's pretty simple but sometimes deceptively difficult to execute.

Your vision can be inspirational, aspirational, and a grounding force all at once. Seeing it and crafting it that way can provide a highly effective foundation for the other elements of balance.

The process of creating a great vision, as is the case with just about everything necessary to become exceptional, is more challenging than it looks. To meet those challenges, here are some things you can (should) do.

Ask a lot of *what-would-it-take* questions. What would it take to make certain that every single strategic objective is aligned with your vision? No exceptions. What would it take to make alignment with and commitment to pursuing your vision a criterion in making your hiring decisions—especially for senior leadership positions? What would it take to correct your current course of action that has taken a detour and bring it back to align with your vision?

And finally, here is a list of the characteristics and practices you can put into place to create and adhere to in order to use your vision in ways that will set you up to become the highest-performing organization possible:

- You have a clearly stated, documented vision. It guides you. It is your North Star.

- Your vision is critically important. You and everyone in your organization is aware of it and believes in it.

- You make certain that your vision and your values are aligned.

- You incorporate your vision into the shaping of your culture. Your cultural behaviors, your reasons for and ways of doing things are always aligned with your vision. If you see your cultural behaviors drifting away from and conflicting with your vision—you make the changes necessary to bring them back into alignment.

- Your vision plays an integral role in helping shape your strategies. You always make certain that your strategic goals align with your vision. If they do not, you alter your strategies to bring them into alignment.

- Your vision and your greater purpose are seamlessly aligned. They are two parts of a united whole.

- You use your vision as one criterion in how you screen and hire new employees. It is important to you that the people you bring into the company will share your vision. If they don't, you usually do not hire them.

If this does not describe your organization as it pertains to your vision, you might want to ask: *What would it take to create, communicate, and keep your vision continually in focus?*

With this first piece of the Mastering Your Balance model in place, you will have planted a solid stake in the ground from which you can continue to build. Let's now focus on the next piece: your values.

CHAPTER 4

Choose Your Core Values

VALUES: *Your unconditional beliefs defined by your consistent behavior in living them over time. Focused inward, they define the character of your culture. Focused outward, they define the experience of your brand.*

Your values are the promise by which you are willing to be judged and held accountable.

B efore we examine how you can create, define, and live the values that best serve your organization, let's look at your personal values and how they came into being.

"By unconscious influence, our character often outwits our purposes. 'What you are speaks so loud I cannot hear what you say,' writes Emerson."
—Charles M. Southgate, Baptist Quarterly Review, 1890

Your personal values were created, shaped, and driven by unconscious beliefs and biases formed as a result of the teachings of your parents and other authority figures during your early life (up to age seven) and firmly etched into your mind by your interpretations of your experiences throughout your late teens and early twenties. In the process of interpretation, you internalized and remembered the events that supported your beliefs while discarding or ignoring experiences that contradicted them.

As a result, the decisions and choices you make about how you behave in the course of living your life result from the beliefs of a seven-year-old child living in the mind and body of a mature adult. Scary.

But wait. You have the ability to change any or all of those values—if you choose to. How?

Leading-edge research findings in neuroscience tell us we are capable of rewiring our brains at the rate of about 18 percent per month—if we commit to the effort to do it. It's accomplished through a process called neuroplasticity: the rewiring of brain circuits to embrace new beliefs/values and discard the old ones. That means we are capable of choosing and changing our values and the behaviors that make them come alive—if we want to. Brain science also tells us that the potential percentage rate of change remains the same at any age. In other words, you are never too old or too set in your ways to change.

We're able to change our thinking, our beliefs, our behaviors, and our results throughout our lifetimes. The old adage that "you can't teach an old dog new tricks" is simply not true. Think about it. It is possible to completely reinvent yourself in a relatively short period of time—if you choose to. You do not have to remain locked in a self-created prison of beliefs that do not serve you well.

WHAT ARE VALUES?

Let's now focus on the present and look at what values truly are and how you can select and live the ones that best serve you.

Every person has values. Every company has values. Values are, in and of themselves, neither good nor bad; they simply reflect the beliefs you choose to live. For example, ISIS has values. The mafia has values. Not all organizations' values have a moral compass that is considered desirable by our society. Most of us have witnessed some organizations that live in ways that demonstrate that their values are greed, money, and power. That's not illegal—until and unless those values carry the organization's actions beyond the limits of our laws. Then all hell breaks loose. People are outraged. *"How could they do that?"* They blatantly disregarded their values. No, they didn't; they just went further in living their values than the law allows.

There are two fundamental truths you should use in determining your values. First, your values are a matter of choice. You are free to choose values that are or can be aligned with all the other elements of balance. Second, there is a strong body of research that shows choosing values that define the behaviors by which your run your business *and* serve as your moral compass will yield significantly better financial, cultural, and strategic benefits—in the long run.

Espousing morally acceptable values and living them are two different things. I think we've all heard variations of the familiar messages put out by organization leaders in every area of our society regarding their values. Here's a summary composite:

Our values guide our behavior. Our values inspire us to conduct ourselves in accordance with their meaning and their message. Our values serve to shape our behavior and remind us to live our lives and conduct our business as they dictate. Our values strengthen and inspire us to live them, because they are the foundation of our success. Our values guide us to achieving our mission. We encourage everyone to hold themselves accountable for living our values.

As long as your values are intended to encourage, guide, suggest, remind, and inspire you—they will not work as intended (if, in fact, it is your true intention to live them under any and all circumstances).

Here's why. Guides and reminders turn values into being mere suggestions. They are toothless. They are no match for the seductive forces that convince people at all levels to, at least temporarily, abandon stated values in favor of aberrant behaviors that address specific situations in seemingly more effective ways—things such as the demands of seemingly costly crises, achieving short-term financial goals that tempt you to bend (or break) the rules, and the allure of lucrative opportunities that appear out of nowhere and promise immediate riches. All those irresistible diversions appear to demand that you, at least, put your values on hold. Don't forget about them, just suspend them for a while. You'll come back to them, just as soon as you clean up the crisis, or meet short-term shareholder demands for increased wealth, or cash in on the unforeseen bonanza dropped in your lap.

Do it once—it's an anomaly, no harm done. Do it twice—a pattern is emerging, and you need to pay attention and investigate. Do it the third time—you can kiss your stated values goodbye. They will become selective, situational, and inconsistent. Even if your intentions remain good, your culture is wise to your pattern. You've been corrupted. What would it take to make living your values become a nonnegotiable reality?

The only thing that makes your values work to their potential is for you to make living them a requirement. The results of behavior are more powerful than the most eloquent words of intention.

The mechanisms that enforce that requirement must be in place, with universal, measurable accountability for living them. There must be positive, meaningful recognition when people do, and immediate, situationally appropriate responses when people do not. Period.

There is a lot of complexity to all of that. You will read about it in the next two chapters. But I want to give you some context for determining how and why to create a set of values that will serve you well, and that you can apply in ways that will best enable you to build the foundation that will maximize your potential.

WHEN CONDUCT CONFLICTS WITH VALUES

To illustrate how values become suggestions for which no one is held accountable (except after the fact, when the transgressions become too egregious), here are two examples of companies whose conduct became a mockery of their stated values.

Volkswagen is one. Part of its mission/values states the following: *We assume responsibility regarding the environment, safety, and social issues. We act with integrity and build on reliability, quality, and passion as the foundation of our work.*

However, VW consciously and purposely violated laws governing air pollution created by the emissions its diesel cars produced. Those cars could not compete if they had to comply with the pollution standards in force. So, VW purposely cheated by engineering its cars to be compliant when tested, but during normal use they emitted pollutants that were up to forty times above the legal limit. It began this practice in 2006 (or perhaps earlier). In 2015, when it finally got caught, its CEO apologized, sort of. He publicly said, *"I personally am deeply sorry that we have broken the trust of our customers and the public."* The cost of its misconduct is, so far, approaching $30 billion. It has a special reserve fund set aside to cover those kinds of "missteps." The fund had a balance of $34 billion. VW was prepared to pay the cost without missing a beat.

Volkswagen legitimized criminal conduct as a normal business activity, executed to pursue financial and strategic goals. The cost of getting caught appears as a line item on its financial statements. This time, however, it suffered additional costs. Its CEO was forced to resign. As of this writing, he is facing criminal charges that could carry a prison sentence. A senior engineer took one for the team, as he was sentenced to seven years in prison. Unfortunate. But it's just collateral damage. There is no hard evidence yet that VW will live its stated values moving forward, although it did promise to obey the law. However, it is easy to see that without a change in its culture that makes living its values a monitored requirement, it's just a matter of time before its next misadventure goes too far.

Wells Fargo—which was a vision failure as well—is another chilling example. Here are its stated values:

- **What's right for customers.** We place customers at the center of everything we do. We want to exceed customer expectations and build relationships that last a lifetime.

- **People as a competitive advantage.** We strive to attract, develop, motivate, and retain the best team members—and collaborate across businesses and functions to serve customers.

- **Ethics.** We're committed to the highest standards of integrity, transparency, and principled performance. We do the right thing, in the right way, and hold ourselves accountable.

- **Diversity and inclusion.** We value and promote diversity and inclusion in all aspects of business and at all levels. Success comes from inviting and incorporating diverse perspectives.

- **Leadership.** We're all called to be leaders. We want everyone to lead themselves, lead the team, and lead the business—in service to customers, communities, team members, and shareholders.

With these values as its declared foundation, over a period of time that by some accounts began in 2011, people in its retail division opened an estimated 3.5 million bank and credit card accounts—without notifying their customers. The fraud was discovered in 2016. During the ensuing investigation, 5,300 midlevel employees were fired. The CEO was forced to resign.

He had to give up $41 million in stock options and was forced to give back an additional $28 million of his earnings. The senior vice president in charge of the division was ousted (it was officially called retirement) and had to forfeit a combined total of $67 million in previous earnings and stock options. A number of states stopped doing business with Wells Fargo. It is now required, by law, to curtail its growth until it cleans up its mess and fixes its culture. Congressional investigations continue to this day. As I write this, the current CEO (recently promoted from within), under pressure from Congress, has just announced his resignation. The list of investigations and sanctions goes on. One current estimate of Wells Fargo's out-of-pocket costs exceeds $3 billion. Its culture remains a confused, dysfunctional mess.

What possessed Wells Fargo's leaders—at several levels in the organization—to abandon the bank's stated values and do the reprehensible things they did? Only they know for certain. I do know, however, there are some people (very smart people) who still think values—like vision—are soft and squishy, touchy-feely concepts that have no place in running a business. They argue that values are intangible and impossible to measure, and they get in the way of the hardball leadership styles needed to succeed in business.

It is common for people to discredit things they don't understand or are not skilled at. I cannot fathom how $3 billion can be seen as touchy-feely. Can you? Firing 5,300 people is more than collateral damage. Being forced to operate under a government-imposed, no-growth mandate until this mess is cleaned up is not soft and squishy—it's having a devastating effect on morale and earnings growth.

These are but two headline-grabbing examples. There are thousands of companies of all sizes, government agencies, and nonprofit organizations that have experienced the effects of stating one set of values and either abandoning them, suspending them, or simply living by a different set.

The point of all this is that *the long-term business interests of every company are best served when they live a set of values that contain a solid moral compass.*

SAMPLE VALUES TO PONDER

This is not as easily implemented as it might seem. Morality in business has always rested on a precarious perch. The pressures to compromise morally aligned values can be relentless and compelling. Rationalizations that justify making values situational can seem too alluring to resist. Some companies have gone so far as to define the limits of morality as *anything you can do without going to prison.*

Yet, while often difficult, it can be done. Over many years of hands-on experience, observations, real-life encounters, and reading, I have seen a handful of values that have proven to be highly effective in achieving outstanding and sustainable results.

These values are examples. I am not saying you must adopt these specific values as your own, or these are the only values that will help you achieve the kinds of successes of which I speak. But for our purposes in this discussion, they will illustrate what is possible, what works, how the values you live seamlessly connect with the other elements of balance and affect outcomes, and how you can adapt your own values in ways that can make your organization and your life more measurably successful. Doing this is an important step in Mastering Your Balance.

Here are the values I will be using, along with brief definitions of what I believe are their meanings:

- **Adaptability:** *Search for what's needed now. Then do it. The past and the present are not divine predictors of the future.*

- **Authenticity:** *Be the best version of the real you.*

- **Humility:** *Give others the sense of their own dignity.*

- **Integrity:** *Keep your commitments. Do the right thing.*

- **Respect:** *Treat others as people.*

- **Deliver great brand experiences:** *Your brand is a widely held set of beliefs and expectations as to what you deliver and how you deliver it, validated by the experiences of everyone with whom you interact.*

- **Alignment with your greater purpose:** *You have a legacy goal, that special something that takes you beyond material wealth and defines how you make the world a better place. You must continuously connect your actions to achieving that goal.*

Here's what makes these values actionable and effective. They all speak to behaviors and outcomes that are measurable and for which you can hold people accountable. Bear in mind that the kind of measurability I refer to is not the line item, quantifiable data presented numerically on income statements and other performance reports. These values in action can be observed in behavioral contexts that lend themselves to productive discussions.

Those discussions can reveal if people's behavior is not aligned with your company's values, and the appropriate changes needed to correct them. They touch all the elements aimed at Mastering Your Balance explored in this book, and they range from the most mundane everyday interactions to the highest level of decision-making by senior executive leaders, extending up to the boardroom.

There is no universal agreement, however, as to how these kinds of values, together with your ability to hold people accountable for living them, work in real life. Some would argue that people's personal values are indelibly ingrained in them. They cannot change. If those values happen to align with the company's, that's great. If not, then they will live their personal values—no matter if their employer's values might dictate to the contrary.

But as I explained earlier, there is more and more scientific evidence being developed every day by neuroscientists around the world that invalidates that argument. We are in the early stages of learning just how neuroplasticity can unlock more of the untapped potential for adaptability that lies within us.

The facts tell us that every leader of every organization can choose to embrace and live a set of values that aligns with its vision, culture, strategies, and greater purpose. And they can make those values come alive as requirements for living, and not mere suggestions leaders can only *hope* most people will live, most of the time, in most situations—when they remember.

Our preexisting beliefs come from our thoughts about what we have been taught, what we've experienced, and how we have interpreted our experiences. But our thoughts don't own us—unless we allow them to. Our thoughts don't define us—unless we allow them to. We are not imprisoned or limited by our thoughts—unless we allow that to become our unchangeable reality.

Our human experience—yours and mine—emanates from *awareness*. The keener and broader our awareness, the more open, creative, wise, adaptive, and accepting of diversity we are. Awareness enables us to see possibilities and opportunities not visible to rigid minds operating in outmoded cultures that cling to counterproductive traditions. Awareness enables us to choose values that work today and will lead us to greater success in the future.

MANIFESTING A VALUES-DRIVEN REALITY

The benefits of creating that values-driven reality can manifest in several ways—all of them good:

- When you articulate your values, you create expectations—from all of your constituencies, internal and external. Those expectations can only be met through your actions.

- When your actions align with your words, you become *authentic*.

- When you are seen as authentic, you will earn *respect*.

- Over time, and in a variety of situations, if you continue to earn respect, you will be seen as having a high degree of *integrity*.

- When you are respected, and are seen as a person of high integrity, you become *trustworthy*. More people will choose to *trust* you.

- And *trust precedes trade*. Metaphorically speaking, we can look at trade as the consummate transaction between you and your ultimate consumer. It can take the shape of something experiential, like the trust needed between a police department and the people in the communities it serves. Or it can be commercial, like the trust needed between Wells Fargo and the customers it serves.

All of this might sound like simple common sense. It might seem pedantic to even write something so basic. But look around. Wells Fargo is a large, global company with highly educated, sophisticated, experienced people running it. They presumably know this stuff. And yet—they completely abandoned these simple components of success—to the tune of $3 billion in costs to date and counting. Police departments around the country are failing to build the trust needed with the communities they serve to deliver the safety and quality of life our society needs and our people deserve. They, too, have ignored the basics. Basics matter.

Large organizations with recognizable names whose actions generate sizable impacts make headlines with their missteps. But the same kinds of actions, the same opportunities to maximize potential and reach levels of greatness, get squandered every day by thousands of smaller companies and the people who lead them. Perhaps your company might be one of them.

But what about examples from companies that have chosen to adopt and live a set of values that contain a moral compass and strive to make them their brand and cultural reality?

Here are Starbucks's core values:

- Creating a culture of warmth and belonging, where everyone is welcome *(aligns with delivering great brand experiences)*

- Acting with courage, challenging the status quo, and finding new ways to grow our company and each other *(adaptability)*

- Being present, connecting with transparency, dignity, and respect *(dignity, respect, and humility)*

- Delivering our very best in all we do, holding ourselves accountable for results *(integrity)*

- We are performance-driven, through the lens of humanity *(authenticity)*

This is Starbucks's vision: *"To establish Starbucks as the premier purveyor of the finest coffee in the world while maintaining our uncompromising principles while we grow."*

Its values do not explicitly connect to its vision. Yet the behaviors it commits to living as described in its values are clearly aligned with the experiences it must deliver as it moves toward its vision.

Here are Zappos's core values:

- Deliver WOW through service *(aligns with delivering great brand experiences)*

- Embrace and drive change *(adaptability)*

- Create fun and a little weirdness *(delivering a great brand experience)*

- Be adventurous, creative, and open-minded *(adaptability)*

- Pursue growth and learning *(adaptability)*

- Build open and honest relationships with communication *(authenticity and respect)*

- Build a positive team and family spirit *(respect)*

- Do more with less *(adaptability)*

- Be passionate and determined *(adaptability and delivering great brand experiences)*

- Be humble *(humility)*

Here is Zappos's vision: *"Delivering happiness to customers, employees and vendors."*

I can look at Zappos's vision and think it does not sound particularly grand or aspirational, or imagine a potential far beyond what it currently possesses. But it's easy to keep it top of mind. It's easy to connect the dots between its performance and its vision. And its values are clearly aligned with delivering happiness while not losing sight of its performance objectives in the process.

We can look at both of these companies' core values and probably cite personal experiences where someone working there did not exhibit one or more of them. That is a continuous challenge with having a scalable model. But it is undeniable that they have achieved steady growth in size, earnings, and market value for an extended period of time. They have experimented with new ideas—and some of those experiments did not turn out well. That comes with being creative.

For the most part, both companies have solid reputations, loyal customer followings, and no scandals, except for a serious incident at a Starbucks in Philadelphia in April 2018. In a Philadelphia store, two black men were arrested for asking to use the bathroom while waiting for a third guest before they made a purchase. Starbucks's initial apology was too tepid. Senior leadership stepped up their game. They fired the store manager who called the police. Both the chairman and the CEO got directly involved and issued personal apologies to the victims. They closed 8,000 stores for a half-day to conduct racial bias training for all their employees in a sincere effort to improve. That specific problem involved cultural issues: conscious and unconscious racial bias. That reality exists not only at Starbucks, but throughout the US. The significant part of that case was that Starbucks, at the most senior leadership level in the company, did not attempt to minimize the seriousness of the problem or to excuse the behavior of that store manager and any other employees who might fail to do the right thing. It's not perfect, but it's probably better than most.

And that's the point. From time to time, problems will occur. Transgressions will take place. Customer trust will be on trial in the court of public opinion. What matters most is how the company's leaders respond, what is done to address and correct the issue, and how the people involved are held accountable. Starbucks did not hide, misrepresent, or deny responsibility. Compare that to how so many organizations respond to a variety of transgressions—sexual harassment, race- or religion-based discrimination, workplace violence, and more—whose fundamental causes can be traced to simply not living their values. Night and day.

GUIDELINES TO HELP CHOOSE YOUR VALUES

Here are three guidelines I have used with great success in choosing values that can help you achieve greater success:

- **Alignment.** It is imperative that your values align with your vision, culture, strategies, and greater purpose. The behaviors those values demand must help take you where you want to go. Less than perfect alignment will create a kind of friction that will diminish your productivity, create disruptive stress, make it more difficult (or impossible) to achieve ambitious goals, cause you to lose focus and make bad decisions, and reduce your profitability.

    - Choose values that align with the kinds of behavioral experiences you want to deliver to your customers, everyone in your organization, and all of your other stakeholders.

- The values you select must align with the ways in which you require your culture to behave and achieve. If the two do not align, select values that express the ways in which you want your culture to operate. Then, fix your culture. That is a tall order that I'll address in the chapter on culture.

- If your chosen values mandate behaviors that don't align with the execution of plans needed to achieve your strategic objectives, you will create conflict. It's the kind of conflict that will tempt people to abandon your values to achieve strategic goals. If people give in to that temptation, you will have just become another Wells Fargo.

• **Measurability.** You must be able to determine whether people are or are not living your values with a clarity that enables you to confront the people involved with unarguable truths about their behavior when they slip up.

- The metrics of measurement will be behavioral. You must be able to demonstrate how someone's behavior conflicted with the meaning and intent of one or more of your values. You must be able to discuss and come to an agreement that a person has failed to live your values; everyone involved must agree that specific corrective behaviors can be implemented and are executable.

— Measurability must be possible at every level of behavior and interaction, in every facet of your business, from the highest levels of leadership to the most mundane, everyday activities.

- **Accountability.** Once you are satisfied that your values are properly aligned with all the elements of balance and they meet the two criteria above, you must make certain the means and methods employed to hold people accountable can, in fact, be communicated to everyone, executed throughout the organization, and be universally applied.

  — The time needed and the methods used to hold people accountable must be ever-present in ways that elevate everyone's conscious awareness, and at the same time, do not become a distraction from the focus and energy needed to operate your business. You want to create awareness without being obsessive.

  — There are no sacred cows. Everyone, without exception, is held to the same standards of behavior and responsibility about how and how well you live your values.

  — That is no small feat, but it is doable. And it's what separates the elite performers from the people for whom values remain a mere suggestion.

We've looked at a couple of examples of companies that have clearly abandoned their stated values and incurred catastrophic costs—costs they arguably would never have incurred had they just believed in and acted on what they promised the world they were committed to doing. So, were their values ever real, or were they merely part of a PR campaign? How do they regain the trust of their constituents?

We've also looked at two companies who have, for the most part, articulated and lived a set of values that have played a large part in their sustained growth and success. They're not perfect (no one is), but they clearly take their values seriously. And people are held accountable for living them.

These examples are useful illustrations. What's really important, however, is what *you* can do. We've looked at what underpins the process of choosing values that have the potential of significantly improving your quest toward Mastering Your Balance and increasing your growth.

Now, let's examine what you must do to create values that support a truly values-driven organization—one in which everyone is held measurably accountable for living them.

VALUES AND HIGH-PERFORMANCE EXECUTION

Earlier in this chapter, I laid out four things you must have in place in determining your values:

- You are best served when you live a set of values that contains a moral compass.

- Your values are not negotiable. True values cannot be situational or conditional.

- Your values must be behaviorally measurable to hold everyone accountable for living them.

- Any set of values that serves merely as a guide, or a source of inspiration, is toothless. They will not achieve their potential value in helping you attain ambitious goals.

Over years of leading and consulting, I have found the highest-performing teams and organizations applied three principles in succeeding to make their chosen values thrive throughout their organization. These principles contributed to help Master Your Balance, maximize productivity, and achieve ambitious goals. Here they are:

- **Existence.** We know precisely what our values are. We have written definitions of what our values mean in a way that provides a roadmap for behavior in terms of how people should live our values.

- **Awareness.** Our values are posted prominently throughout our facilities. Everyone knows what our values mean and what behaviors are required to live them.

- **Execution.** Everyone in our company knows they are expected to live our values—all the time, in every situation and every interaction—with everyone inside and outside our company. We have a formal system in place to make every person measurably accountable for living our values. We also regularly acknowledge people who go above and beyond to uphold our values.

Now I trust you have a sense of what values mean and how you can go about choosing the ones that will best serve you. In the next two chapters, I'll explore what it will take to breathe life and power into your values by making people measurably accountable for living them. In doing that, you will replace toothless suggestions with an effective foundation for creating a high-performing culture.

CHAPTER 5

Practice Values-Driven Leadership

Values-driven leadership is the art of transforming your values from being suggestions to being requirements that demand accountability. Universal accountability gives you the behavioral consistency needed for scalable success.

Although the benefits of measurable accountability are intellectually inarguable, this is the thorniest of all the elements of Mastering Your Balance to harness, apply, and sustain. There is a fundamental explanation for why that is so.

For individuals, *holding everyone in the organization equally accountable conflicts with human nature.* Let me explain. Humans are, by nature, tribal. Our brains are wired that way. Tribalism is the default setting for our behavior. It unfolds like this.

Tribal leaders value their power. They work to protect and expand that power. They also value loyalty. Loyal people help them retain and increase their power. Tribe members, on the other hand, value acceptance. Behavioral privileges given by their leader as perks, to people or groups of people the leader wants to favor, are signs of acceptance. All of it translates to mutual loyalty. Over centuries, a lot of titles and structures have changed, but our hardwiring has remained constant. Tribal behavior remains the default, normal expression of human nature. In that mode, leaders will hold some people more accountable than others. Therein lies the foundation for double standards and sacred cows.

> "HE THAT IS GOOD FOR MAKING EXCUSES IS
> SELDOM GOOD FOR ANYTHING ELSE."
>
> —*Anonymous*

Since uniform accountability conflicts with human nature, that begs a bigger question. If *everyone* cannot be held to the same standard of accountability, why should *anyone* be held to such a standard? It seems unfair. And if no one is held accountable for living your values, isn't an attempt to define your values a waste of time? No, it's not. To tell the world you do not subscribe to a prescribed set of beliefs and you do not have a moral compass would be shameful. It could threaten your perceived qualifications to be a leader.

Here's what most people (and organizations) do instead. They start by accepting the self-limiting belief that they cannot hold everyone to the same standard of accountability. Then they try to reconcile the conflict between selective vs. universal accountability. They achieve reconciliation by declaring their values to be a set of *behavioral guidelines, guiding principles,* or something similar. In doing that, they hold themselves accountable for *trying.* That allows for situational lapses, where they simply forget their values and allow the sacred cows to not be bound by them. The organization's values might be aspirational—above the level of ordinary, daily human interaction. Or they might be focused on day-to-day behaviors at every level. They could be a mix of both. Whatever they are, they share the same deficiency. They are used in ways that do not require or enforce individual and universal measurable accountability. The tribal characteristics of human nature prevail.

When you allow that, you compromise your organization's ability to Master Your Balance. Scalability of size and mastery of performance become diminished by what we call *normal human nature*—one of the greatest copouts there is to avoid being accountable.

Let's take a closer look at how this plays out, starting with your culture. As you make it clear, through your actions, that certain people will not be held accountable for behavior that violates your values, consider the peripheral effects on all the people who feel less favored.

Do you sense that otherwise good employees do what is minimally acceptable and no more? Are they unlikely to go the extra mile to achieve goals? Are their communications and teamwork with "privileged" people less than stellar? Is the daily energy civil but not warm? Does the chill in the air affect how your customers are treated by the "underprivileged" people in your organization? If your behavior around privilege is hierarchal in nature, does that exacerbate a we-versus-they cultural norm that inhibits the free flow of information and diminishes team effectiveness? Are cliques being formed between the haves and have-nots? Is employee turnover a bit too high, and are you losing too many of your best employees?

If you have allowed this condition to exist in your organization, I'm betting you can identify even more symptoms than those I just mentioned. If it has existed for a long time (multiple years), you may be blind to it. You don't even recognize that the results of your unwritten cultural norms are anything out of the ordinary—certainly nothing that diminishes the effectiveness of your people to achieve outstanding results. If double standards of accountability have been going on for many years, consider the possibility (actually, the reality) that your benchmark for greatness may define very good, but it falls short of being exceptional. You are selling yourself short. You're not realizing your full potential.

LAPSES IN LIVING YOUR VALUES

Now let's examine the lapses in living your values you may experience when they result from a conflict between your values and normal *human nature*—especially those values that reflect your moral compass. They typically occur when you are confronted with crises or opportunities that seem to demand you suspend your values to address a specific purpose for a defined period of time. You would do well to look at the peripheral effects of those lapses, especially on your culture and on your ability to execute the strategies and tactics you employ to address those situations.

Temporarily putting your values aside to achieve a goal that requires actions that violate those values raises some important questions (or at least it should). *Do we really believe in our stated values, or are they just window dressing to cover up who we really are? Is the person or group responsible for this lapse authorized to do this, or are they exceeding their authority? If they are violating our values without permission, why are they not held accountable? If they have permission, what possible justification could there have been to grant it? Have we weighed the potential long-term costs of violating our values against the short-term gains we see as justifying our actions? Do the people who approved this operate with a different set of rules than the rest of us? Are they, like the people not held accountable, members of a special class? Are there other ways to achieve our objectives while still living in alignment with our values? And a big one, does the content of our actions erase the character of our beliefs?*

In my experience, the justification for suspending one's values that is most often expressed is, *"Hey, this is the real world. Not everyone plays by the rules. We need to deal with what is, not what we'd like it to be. If we can't do that, we'll be out of business. We'll get back to our values when this situation is past us. So grow up."* Or words to that effect.

The question then becomes, how often and under what circumstances do you find yourself putting your values on the back burner while you deal with whatever? If your bar for justifying deviation is high, if it happens rarely and it is largely based on circumstances beyond your control, you might get a pass in the court of cultural opinion.

If, on the other hand, you often hide your values in the closet and find it easy to rationalize your lapses while you pursue opportunities or manage crises, you may have chosen values that are not really values—they are situational strategies masquerading as values. I am reminded of a statement I heard many years ago from the CEO of a global glass distribution company during a meeting at its headquarters in Johannesburg,

South Africa. *"These are my principles, by God. If you don't like them—I have others."* He was joking when he said it, but his message is too often true. The question is, is it true for your organization?

I have seen too many organizations unconsciously descend down this slippery slope to a point where cultural behavior regarding living in accordance with stated values in the course of running the company has become a coincidence. Living their values is assumed but often never consciously considered. Short-term results (mostly measured in financial terms) are all that matter.

Once again, the Wells Fargo debacle with its long-term costs serves as the poster child for the short-sighted blindness (some would say greed) that drove smart people to do dumb things. I was never privy to the inner workings of Wells Fargo. So, like many of you, all I know is what I read and heard in the various media accounts. It's understandably damning. Over the years, as a customer/client of Wells Fargo, I came to know several Wells Fargo executives and managers. I believed they were good, smart, ethical people. They never acted in ways that gave me any doubts about their own or the bank's integrity.

Somewhere along the line, however, something went terribly wrong—not for everyone—but for enough high-ranking executives and employees so as to destroy trust to such a degree that some members of Congress don't believe any insider is qualified to right their ship. The needle moved from serious to dire. That cannot be explained away as a temporary lapse.

I believe the Wells Fargo circumstances offer a valuable lesson for the rest of us. It is this. Once you lose conscious awareness of the fact that your goal is no longer aligned with your values, or you know it, but you don't care, you no longer own that goal—the goal owns you. You are enslaved. If the goal is big and demanding, and it requires significant financial and human capital to execute it, the downward slope can become a freefall.

Did the leaders at Wells Fargo have alternatives? Again, I only know what I read, but it seems they did. They created an initiative: sell additional products and services to existing customers. Smart concept. The easiest people to sell to are people who are already your customers. They trust you. You've passed the first requirement in commerce; trust must precede trade. Now you just need to create or address a perceived need with a viable solution, and you're home free.

Here's where it got dicey. To convincingly present the need and the solution takes a certain level of knowledge and applied skill. Too few employees had the requisite skills to make the initiative viable. More training, perhaps? That would take longer than desired. Set lower performance goals and ramp them up as people got more proficient? Unacceptable. Leaders wanted more, faster. Threats of job loss might work. Do it. Pressure, pressure, and more pressure. The unwritten message was delivered: succeed by any means necessary. Loopholes in the system allowed bank employees to open accounts without notifying their customers. Holy shit. That's illegal. Do it anyway—or lose your job. And when you're fired for incompetence, try getting another job in banking.

When the "game" was discovered, and heads began to roll, some of the senior leaders blamed a bunch of unqualified or underqualified staff people (about 5,300 of them) for improperly opening accounts because they could not otherwise meet their sales goals. Why would they hire unqualified people in the first place? Why would they not determine, in advance, the skill levels needed to achieve their goals—do a GAP analysis (measuring the gap between where they were and where they wanted to go, and determine what resources they would need to get there)? Deficiencies in skill levels and the need for training should have come to light at that point if they hadn't already. But training would take time and cost money. Cheating was cheaper and faster.

All of this illustrates my point. These acts were committed by smart, experienced people, people who knew the bank's values, people who were seasoned veterans. If they could have stepped back from the precipice, taken a deep breath, analyzed and clearly thought through what they were about to do, and wisely considered and executed alternative approaches that would have addressed the same objectives but in ways that aligned with their values, just imagine how different the results would have been. It's mind-boggling, but only in hindsight. In the heat of the moment, they were lost, they were held captive by their self-conceived trap. In that state, soft and fluffy values could be dismissed as the fairy tale delusions of naïve children who did not know of and could not compete in the dog-eat-dog competitive world of big business.

No one is immune from those temptations, including you. Wells Fargo was not the first and won't be the last to fall prey.

But you have the opportunity to learn the lessons it taught all of us and never travel that trajectory of tragedy.

Wells Fargo (and others) represent an epic extreme. For every transgression on that scale, there are thousands of smaller, non-life-threatening encounters in which values clash with the perceived realities of life. And there seems to be ample experiential support to establish that tribal behavior and life's compromising realities make true accountability for living a defined set of values contradictory to human nature. Accountability is impossible to achieve at any reasonable scale. It is naïve to believe otherwise. If you believe that to be true, you'd be wrong. Well, not entirely wrong. But wrong enough to prevent you from achieving significant improvements in performance. Here's why.

Creating and enforcing universal accountability is not an all-or-nothing game. Achieving and sustaining balance is an organic process in which everything affects everything else. The peripheral effects of any action can become a force multiplier and create a disproportional effect on the things they touch. And the higher up in the leadership hierarchy an example of accountability occurs, the more influential it is and the more widespread its effects will be felt.

VALUES AND MEASURABLE ACCOUNTABILITY

It is important to note that when I use the term *measurable accountability*, I am referring to *behavioral* actions as the foundation of measurability. Overt behaviors are observable and connectible to the results they generate. Those actions don't show up on any operational or financial performance report. But they are just as tangible. If I call a customer or colleague an asshole, we don't need an evidence-based study to know it will have a measurable effect that will extend beyond the people directly involved.

Here is a simple story to illustrate the point. It's a true story involving one of my past clients that demonstrates the outsized effects of a single act. All the names have been changed for privacy purposes.

The company was in the graphic design business. It produced all the display ads for a major newspaper in a large city. Almost all the artwork to build the ads was done between 7:00 p.m. and 5:00 a.m. and electronically sent to the newspaper to meet the printing deadline. One hundred twenty graphic artists worked all night at a breakneck pace to produce the ads. Speed and accuracy were critical. Finding qualified people willing to work under that kind of pressure at those odd hours was challenging.

We had recently completed a process in which the company's leaders chose and defined its eight core values. Everyone in the company was introduced to the values, how they were defined and how everyone was expected to be held measurably accountable for living them. Everyone signed a document acknowledging their understanding of and commitment to do just that.

The company had just hired a new graphic artist. Sarah was a young woman with strong academic training and no full-time work experience. She was introduced to the company's values as part of her interview process. She eagerly embraced the prospect of working in a culture with those values.

The CEO, Jim Trainer, worked days. The company had a team of strong operations managers who worked the night shift and handled all production matters. But Jim made it his practice to come in once or twice a month to just hang out on the production floor to keep his finger on the pulse of what was happening and assess the overall energy and passion the company's people had.

Jim showed up one night a few days after Sarah finished her initial training and began working on the production floor. He was not involved in her hiring. He had never met or spoken to her. While standing at one end of the production floor, Jim looked up to see someone at the other end eagerly gesturing for him to come over there. It seemed urgent. As Jim walked quickly toward the person who signaled him, Sarah was walking the other way. Their paths crossed. Jim saw her for the first time. He knew she must be the new person he was told about. She looked at him, smiled, and said, "Hello, Mr. Trainer, it's nice to meet you." Jim smiled back, and since he didn't know her name, he simply said, "Hi, nice to meet you," and kept walking toward his destination.

A simple encounter. Nothing odd about it. Two days later, Jim got an email from Sarah. I'm paraphrasing, but the essence of her message was this.

"When I came to work here, I was excited because you have a defined set of values, and I was told everyone in the company was committed to living them. One of them was respect. You and I

had not met before the other night. But I took the time to look up the names and faces of all the managers and executives and memorize them. When you and I passed each other, I knew your name, but you did not know mine. I felt disrespected. Maybe I'm out of line, and maybe I'm naïve, but I believe I have a right to feel my feelings. And I just wanted you to know. And when I wrote this email, I was afraid to send it because I don't know what will happen. Will I get fired? Will there be some kind of retaliation? Did I make a mistake by coming to work here? I don't know, but I had to tell you how I feel because respect is a big deal to me. Thank you for reading this."

On its face, many leaders would simply see this as the inappropriately naïve behavior of a junior employee who was not familiar with how things work in a business environment. There was clearly no disrespect intended. Some people would just ignore the email and let the chips fall where they may. Some might have written a response that said something like, *"Thank you for your input. I'm sorry you were offended, but I can assure you I meant no disrespect."*

Jim did something different. He set his alarm for midnight that night, awoke, and came into the office. He found Sarah and asked her to get permission to take a break and come into his office. She did. Jim apologized to Sarah. He apologized for not respecting her by not taking the time to learn and call her by her name. He apologized for not demonstrating the company's value of respect. He thanked her for having the courage to speak up and reiterated that when it came to living their values, there was no hierarchy in the organization. Everyone was equally accountable. Especially him. And he reassured her that she made the right decision to come to work there. Then he asked her to tell him more about herself, so he could come to know her better. She did. Their meeting lasted thirty minutes. Sarah thanked him and went back to work.

Jim thought the incident was private and resolved, so there would be no repercussions. He was wrong. Other graphic artists working on the production floor that night noticed Sarah had been gone. They grilled her. She told them how everything went down and how much more she respected Mr. Trainer (everyone else called him Jim) and the company, and how its values were not just well-intentioned words—they really mattered. Word spread. This time, however, unlike most grapevine news that spreads quickly, the news wasn't bad; it was good. The message was clear to everyone. Jim's conduct proved he walked the talk, and the company's values were real. People loved it. Morale, already good, got better. Productivity improved. Who knew?

What exactly was it that made that meeting so productive and created the positive vibes that resonated throughout the company? The point of resonance with the employees began with Sarah's account of the meeting to her coworkers. What was in how she told it that gave it that kind of juice?

When Jim met with Sarah, after reading her email and understanding her perspective, he could have delivered a factually correct, logical explanation for his behavior, his busy schedule, the assumed sense of urgency in walking quickly to the people who asked him to come over. He could have told Sarah more about how hierarchal structures typically work in companies and how it was normal and natural that he would not know Sarah's name that soon in her tenure. He could have gone further and nicely told her that her feelings about not being respected were naïve and overly sensitive (in other words, grow up and stop acting like a child).

If he had done that, Sarah might have seen the error in her ways, taken Jim's message constructively, used it as a learning moment, and achieved the same result. Hypothetically possible. In my experience and in listening to other leaders over many years, however, that would rarely happen. It almost always would have produced negative outcomes. Sarah would most likely have felt demeaned, less than. Her account of the meeting to her coworkers would have reflected that. That, in turn, would have influenced the tone of the grapevine communication to the other employees. Jim's good intentions would have yielded a less than ideal outcome.

This, though, is more than the story of being accountable; it is also a story about empathy. Jim understood and addressed the issue through Sarah's perspective and acted from that place. He believed the facts-of-life realities that would help Sarah mature would happen naturally, through her experiences over a reasonable time. Was this an almost fictional story that reads like a fairy tale? A pristine picture of purity that never happens in real life? No. To be sure, it is rare, but only for one reason. Because few people operate the way Jim Trainer did. Jim did not answer to Sarah, or in his case, to anyone else in the company. He answered only to the face in his mirror. On his own, he made a conscious decision to hold himself accountable to a set of values. His reasoning was simple. If he wasn't accountable, how could he demand that others must be? It did not matter that Sarah was naïve, maybe overly sensitive, and lacked an experienced understanding of how most businesses function. Through unfocused eyes, she was trying to live and experience the company's values. How could he possibly put her down for that? So he didn't.

Fast forward eighteen months. Sarah was promoted to department manager. She proved to be a darn good one. She was also one of the strongest role models in the company for living its values. That further served to help make accountability a universal cultural norm.

Being empathetic, as Jim was, is not just a business leadership skill; it's a life skill. Everything contained in the story above applies to the interactions in your life—with family members, significant others, friends, and strangers. You are always the leader of you. Empathy always begins and ends with you. And the choice to learn the skill, embrace it, and apply it is always yours to make.

Admittedly, the company in my example was small. It operated in one location. You might think its experience is not scalable. But large companies are not monolithic, hierarchal structures that live with a singular pulse, one voice, one set of cultural norms. Sometimes, they even have more than one set of values. Companies are made up of hundreds, even thousands of cultural pods. Each pod has its own microculture. It is typically true that there is a continuous effort to make the pods speak and act with one voice, one culture, one set of values, one overarching list of strategic goals, and a singular mission and purpose. Yet, it is also true that it doesn't always work that way. Complexity gets in the way, personally and organizationally. Politics gets in the way. Structure gets in the way. Some organization structures are purposely designed to give the most senior leaders plausible deniability for the sins of subordinates. How convenient is that?

I believe measurable accountability is scalable. But only if you want it. Of course, all the factors I stated above (and more) make it challenging, to say the least. The podular makeup of organizations, however, make accountability incrementally effective—and a force multiplier. Establishing universal accountability inside a cultural pod, with its own formally named and situational leaders (leaders without titles), is clearly doable. When you do that, you create a ripple effect that travels outside the bounds of the pod—especially when it has positive effects on the employees involved.

In the next chapter, I'll lay out some additional challenges that make universal accountability difficult. Then, I will talk about how changes in leadership models and win-win interactions provide better approaches to accountability and the improved results that come with it. And I will discuss some practical approaches (i.e., what would it take) to address all the challenges and bring you closer to making measurable accountability a reality.

CHAPTER 6

Refine Your Values-driven Leadership

You cannot be responsible unless you are willing to be accountable.

In the last chapter, I stated three things about behavioral challenges to accountability that bear repeating:

- Holding everyone in the organization equally accountable conflicts with human nature (because we're wired to be tribal).

- If *everyone* cannot be held to the same standard of accountability, why should *anyone* be held to such a standard? It seems unfair.

- Most people believe the enormity of certain real-world challenges makes it a practical impossibility to hold people accountable for living your values.

For some, those three statements would signal the end of the discussion about universal accountability. Accept reality and move on. Hopefully, you are not in that group. While it is true that equal, universal accountability all the time in every situation might be an idealistic goal to achieve, it is also true that it is possible to constantly reach for it, and by doing that, measurably improve your organizational balance and reach new heights of performance.

In my experience, many leaders who achieve a level of *good* seem satisfied to sustain that level. Their goal is to preserve the status quo. It's not a bad place to be, and staying there can be rationalized in several ways. It is also my experience that those who want more than just good, and those who have already become exceptional, are never content to remain static. They are always looking for ways to improve. True champions are never complacent.

> "ACCOUNTABILITY IS THE MEASURE OF A
> LEADER'S HEIGHT."
> —*Jeffrey Benjamin*

To begin our journey toward universal accountability, let's examine the barriers you must overcome to reach that level. In the previous chapter, I addressed two realities that speak to the behavioral pull that draws people to temporarily and situationally abandon their values. One deals with what we know to be our hardwired tribal behavior (normal human nature) that has us creating sacred cows. The other reflects the eternal battle between the desire to live one's values versus the impulse to abandon them (at least temporarily) to successfully address real-world issues. It plays out like this. *When the going gets tough, the tough trash their values.*

CHARACTERISTIC TYPES OF VALUES

Here is a list of the characteristic types of values I have experienced that intentionally or unintentionally invite confusion and obstruct accountability. I'm guessing you have encountered at least some of these obstacles.

- **When your values are aspirational ideals— with fuzzy meanings, subject to multiple interpretations.** Structural idealism comes into play when leaders and followers believe values exist on a higher plane. They are perceived as perfect world ideals lived by perfect people behaving perfectly at the 40,000-foot level. Or they are only connected to behaviors and the results they manifest at a high strategic level. *Aspirational values, in practice, contain tacit permission to fail to live them.* Aspiration is partly viewed as hope. Hopes are sometimes achieved for brief periods but are not sustainable. Therefore, accountability itself can never be more than an ideal—certainly not something people can be expected to practice consistently (or even think about) in their day-to-day conduct at ground level.

  You create behavioral idealism when you have a value and fail to define it in a way that makes its meaning universally understood and interpretable in practical, behaviorally relevant ways that apply to all levels of interaction—from the basement to the boardroom. Take integrity, for example. You might say something like, *we expect our people will be guided by their own moral compass and always act with integrity in everything they do.* When you make the definition of a value sufficiently vague so people can bend its meaning to their preference, you will have eliminated your ability to hold people accountable for living that value. If you make self-accountability the *only* form of behavioral control, you have diminished your chances of having effective organizational accountability. No one I know has ever looked at themselves in the mirror and said, "Your misconduct is epic and harmful. You're fired."

- **When your values are assumptive.** Some people believe values are the basic rules for living you learned as a child from the authority figures in your life: parents, grandparents, teachers, religious leaders, etc. These rules/values are assumed to be universally known by everyone, understood to have a singular meaning embraced by all, and practiced by most, most of the time. No further explanations needed. The Golden Rule, honesty, telling the truth, respecting people, etc.—they are just plain common sense. Right?

  When values are assumed into being, they are typically put on the back burner of awareness and ignored in the day-to-day conduct of everyone's activities and interactions. There is no effort made to connect values to the other elements of balance. There is similarly no explicit or implicit connection made between living those values and outcomes. Failure to live assumed values is almost never seen as the root cause of unintended results. Instead, companies that view values in that light look to policy manuals, written rules, and regulations contained in SOPs (standard operating procedures) as the standards by which they measure performance. They blame a lack of training or systems failures when the rules are not adhered to. Additionally, values are not used to help make hiring decisions, conduct performance evaluations, or align strategies. No need to, because after all, *it's just common sense—let's not overthink this.*

- **When your values are intentionally implicit.** Some leaders have decided that while they may feel values are important, they do not want to put pressure on people to be held individually accountable for living them. Others believe trying to establish personal accountability is subjective and too time-consuming. It distracts people from their jobs and impairs productivity. Implied meanings allow for multiple interpretations and applications of your values. Thus, in turn, they quickly devolve into a passive presence and become suggestions. Accountability, if it exists at all, becomes situational, subjective, and meaningless. Any connection between the values you think you hold and the results you achieve is purely coincidental.

- **When your values are intentionally situational.** This characteristic is more explicit than the one I discussed in the previous chapter. In my earlier depiction, the abandonment of your stated values was at odds with your intentions. If your values are intentionally situational, it reflects the views many people may have, which is that values can and should change as circumstances on the ground warrant. That belief turns your values into strategies. It makes living your values shaped and defined by interpretations as to what you had to do to achieve short-term objectives or to reactively respond to challenges you face. Behaviors are a subjective assessment of whatever is needed at the moment. Immediate results replace wisdom in an either-or scenario constructed to justify actions. True accountability is impossible.

- **When your values depict what you think people want to hear, rather than your true beliefs.** When your values are structurally and behaviorally disingenuous, you have no chance of establishing a culture of accountability. In fact, the more you try, the more seeds of mistrust you will sow. You'd be trying to hold people accountable for something you're not. That is toxic. Nothing good can come of it.

- **When double standards exempt certain people from living your values.** In my experience, this is the most frequently encountered and most problematic challenge of all. Sacred cows come in a variety of breeds, and they are all disruptive: senior leaders who are seen as being above the rules of personal accountability purely due to their positions in the organization, family members who benefit from nepotism, high performers (typically in sales) for whom the rules don't apply—mostly out of fear of ruffling their feathers, employees with political connections (inside and outside the organization) that suggest they are exempt from the rules, employees involved in extracurricular relationships with senior executives, employees who may have damaging information related to senior executives, and other special circumstances unique to your organization.

All of these examples make universal, measurable accountability seem like a practical impossibility. But is it? Let us shift to what factors facilitate accountability, how you can frame your views about accountability more positively and set yourself up to address the magic question: *What would it take to make measurable accountability for living your values a practical reality in your company?*

"RESPONSIBILITY EQUALS ACCOUNTABILITY EQUALS OWNERSHIP. AND A SENSE OF OWNERSHIP IS THE MOST POWERFUL WEAPON A TEAM OR ORGANIZATION CAN HAVE."

—*Pat Summitt*

DOUBLE STANDARDS

We'll start with double standards. The presence of *double standards* deserves its own special focus because it has some unique characteristics that don't necessarily apply to the other challenges.

Let's talk about tribal behavior and its role in making certain "special" people unaccountable for living your values. Tribalistic behavior is a zero-sum game. For me to win, you must lose. And vice versa. From the perspective of making living your values a universal requirement and not a selective suggestion, it looks like this. You compromise accountability for select people by allowing them to ignore your values with impunity. Each compromise results in a tradeoff. You get some perceived immediate reward—achieving a better financial result, avoiding discomfort, or preventing the possible loss of a valuable employee. You also strengthen the bond of loyalty with the affected employees. Those employees support your actions. They comprise your base. In exchange, you are willing to incur an unmeasured longer-term cost, often greater than the immediate gain you realized by suspending your values. In my experience, the long-term cost is rarely even considered. Human nature triggers an instinctive acceptance of a timeworn given: unequal treatment is normal. You remain imprisoned in that box. Deep down, you know you could improve your performance if everyone could be held measurably accountable for living your values. But how? How can you extricate yourself, even if it's only some of the time?

There is a relatively new game in town that contradicts this tribal tradition and its zero-sum behavioral model. It is a win-win collaboration. Human interaction based on inclusion and collaboration is a behavioral model that challenges the notion that human nature is unchangeable. It began to stake its claim for mainstream inclusion in its current form in the 1980s. Although win-win collaboration has been primarily used to resolve conflicts and improve outcomes in a variety of negotiating situations, it has broader applications regarding other kinds of interactions—specifically, making living your values a requirement.

Here's one way to go about replacing zero-sum with collaboration. You can promote accountability as being the new currency of favoritism. You can tell your people you will reward collaboration as a sign of loyalty. Unwillingness, on the other hand, will be interpreted as being disloyal. People who do not collaborate will be privately and explicitly called out. In terms of transforming your own tribal instincts to non-tribal behavior, I see it this way. Adopting a win-win approach to universal accountability is a better way of increasing your power and influence—and the size of your tribe. Win-win approaches can significantly expand the scalability of your business; they can take you well beyond the profitable growth limits imposed by the win-lose foundation of tribalism.

Use accountability in even the smallest and most seemingly unimportant instances when people fail to live your values. By doing that, you accomplish two important goals on the path to transformation: you help establish and maintain continuous top-of-mind awareness regarding your values, how to live them, and how to be responsible for doing so; and you can make responses to lapses become opportunities for performance improvement—not punishment. Good coaches do that all the time.

Just as you call peoples' attention to small lapses, publicly acknowledge and recognize people when they live your values in ways that help bring about good results. Correct in private, reward in public. The need for recognition is perhaps the single most important sign of respect we all share. Using it often, authentically, and sincerely will go a long way toward lifting everyone's desire to live your values.

This is not an easy transition for people who have been allowed to play outside the rules and enjoy special privileges for some time. Your new message will be tested, especially by people who feel they are irreplaceable. In my experience, one high-profile Machiavellian example will often tip the scales of cultural change in your favor. If push comes to shove, and your leadership is tested to its limits, fire one high performer. Let everyone know why. You will have everyone's undivided attention. I don't suggest this cavalierly. I have used it only when I felt there were no other choices. When I did, it worked. Listen to your instincts. Have the courage to follow them.

There are some cases, however, in which there is nothing you can do to change the double standards. I have seen many cases of family members being exempt from all the rules—no matter what. I have also seen a few instances where family members were held to the same or higher standards as everyone else. If they didn't measure up, they weren't necessarily terminated, but they were marginalized and put in positions where they could not be a deterrent to high performance.

Sometimes the rules and restrictions on discipline and individual accountability contained in union contracts make universal adherence to your values highly unlikely. That is typically a long-term issue best handled by building stronger relationships and committing to mutually agreed-upon performance goals with union leaders. In my experience, it has been difficult but at least partially doable in many situations.

Even given all the things you can do to eliminate double standards, in most organizations where they exist, some remnants stubbornly remain. In those situations, they still pose a potent challenge. In those cases, you have three choices:

- Declare that going forward, the playing field will be level for everyone. Eliminate the double standards by decree and decisively act to remove those privileges from people who have them. This option is only for the bravest of the brave. To successfully use this approach, it is imperative you do a good, thorough assessment of the collateral (and unintended) consequences brought on by this significant, traumatic cultural shift. You'll need to have appropriate responses in place to deal with the behavioral fallout.

- Be honest and transparent with everyone who is not a member of a privileged class. Explain life is not fair; you will do your best to make those privileged people want to live your values, but when push comes to shove, there will be some injustices. It's not perfect, but if enough people are accountable, you will still achieve a high level of success.

- Embrace denial. Pretend the privileges don't exist and everyone is and will continue to be treated equally when it comes to living your values. This is your worst possible option. Everyone knows it's total BS. That pretense will undermine any level of trust in leadership by everyone in the organization. It will result in material unintended, costly collateral damage. It is far better to admit to an unpleasant reality than to pretend it does not exist. Denial is always a bad option.

A transition to flatter organization structures can provide great assistance in helping you hold people measurably accountable for living your values. The same can be said for those of you who are creating agile organizations. The very nature of flat and agile organizations demands greater collaboration and less tribalism. Collaborative approaches, shared authority, and situational leadership are just new ways of expanding the size and reach of tribes.

Flat organizations and the resulting demise of traditional, hierarchal chains of command are, for many people, disruptive and therefore uncomfortable. But that discomfort is necessary to achieve acceptable levels of scalability. It is required to increase profitable growth, whether organically, through acquisitions, or by diversification. The realities of these seemingly disruptive shifts from hierarchal command and control to more inclusive models of leadership frame the willingness (or resistance) of traditional leaders to relinquish much of their decision-making authority.

The nature of flat and agile organizations is to push decision-making authority down into the ground levels of an organization. In doing that, much of the traditional power held by senior leaders is distributed to many others who then experience more authority and its accompanying responsibility. It is easier to get people in those positions to embrace the need to be measurably accountable—for their conduct, their choices, and their results—especially when doing so in constructive ways improves their performance and advances their careers. Use that emerging cultural shift to your advantage. Making individual accountability a reality has a positive effect on the organization's performance. A well-designed flat organization will not obviate the need for and the benefits derived from having everyone held measurably accountable for living your values. The case for accountability, however, is usually made easier and becomes more executable.

I will talk more in the next chapter about the benefits of transitioning any culture, regardless of the company's structure, from one of "normal human nature" tribal behavior to one of being more collaborative in all areas of operations and decision-making.

ADDRESSING ACCOUNTABILITY

In dealing with the other challenges listed above that make measurable accountability seem unattainable, there are some common approaches that address all of them, singularly and collectively. Begin with your list of existing values, whether already in existence or newly created. Examine them carefully to see if they are serving you as you intended. Make certain you have defined them in ways that are meaningful and specific to your organization. The definitions should reflect the ways in which you want those values demonstrated through the behavior of everyone in your company. I have seen that in most cases, at the least, you will modify the definitions of certain values. Others you will discard and replace. Then:

- Exhaustively examine how your values align with the real-life challenges and requirements of operating and growing your organization. Do that from both an internal and external perspective—operationally in the way you treat each other, and outward-facing in the way you address your markets/customers and external stakeholders. Are your values designed to deliver the experiences all your constituencies want to receive? If not—fix them.

- Explore and articulate exactly if, how, and to what extent those values can be made behaviorally measurable at every level of human interaction within the context of your organization's culture and the nature of your business.

- If you like the values you have chosen, but you cannot define them in ways that fit the realities of your organization, they are probably situational. As such, they don't rise to the level of being core values. Use them when you can—as appropriate behavioral *strategies*. Know if you try to force them to become your values, they will, at some point, blow up in your face. They will only serve to discredit your organization, label you as a hypocrite, and tarnish your brand. All of those things will cost you dearly. Choose more appropriate values—ones you can commit to live unconditionally.

- Before you make your final decisions as to your choices of values, test them out on opinion leaders from all facets of your business. Your line of questioning should relate to whether or not those values as they are defined, can be measurably lived, are in the organization's best interests, and fit or can be adapted to fit within your cultural norms.

- If they don't fit within your cultural norms and you still want them, you must develop plans for implementing whatever level of cultural adaptation is needed to make those values work for you. If you think your culture will just adapt on its own without any change in leadership style, you are being delusional. It will not work.

If the values you have chosen cannot ultimately meet all of these requirements, go back to square one and choose new ones that do.

This is a tall order. It outlines a process that most organizations don't go through, or they do some but not all of it. Doing it deeply and completely is one of the factors that separate the exceptional from the acceptable. Not doing it is one of the reasons why some organizations find themselves consistently failing to meet ambitious objectives, experiencing unexplained attrition rates by their best people, and often unconsciously lowering their performance standards and growth goals. In the most extreme cases, they find themselves embroiled in a variety of scandals, experience behavior-related public relations disasters that reduce earnings and brand strength, and even end up settling lawsuits bearing catastrophic costs over misconduct directly tied to not living their values. And in almost all those situations, senior leaders deliver rehearsed, carefully worded mea culpas (crafted to avoid further damage) and loudly proclaim that no one could have seen this coming. There's a term for that tactic. It's called BS.

But wait, there's more. Once you know what your values are, what they mean, and how you want your people to live them, there are methods to make living them a reality that we have developed and used and observed and seen work in many companies of all sizes in a variety of industries. They help make people feel that being accountable is a desirable way to be, professionally and personally. They are as follows:

Become a culture of making and keeping commitments. Being accountable rests on a foundation of making, accepting responsibility for, and keeping commitments. Commitments almost always speak to something specific that must be accomplished, whether it is a tangible "thing" or a less tangible change in some behavior. Commitments replace "trying." Commitments say, "I will get this done, no matter what." And there is almost always a date/time and a mutual understanding of what the deliverable will look like. Getting something done, no matter what, is a lot stronger than, "I'll try," or "I'll give it a shot, but I can't promise," or "I think I can do it, but I can't tell you when." Commitments carry with them a measurable context for accountability. Trying does not. I don't know how to hold someone measurably accountable for *trying*. Do you? When you can create a culture of making and keeping commitments, you will have gone a long way toward making accountability a cultural norm.

Constantly ask *what-would-it-take* questions. Early in this book, I told the story of the origin of that question, its importance, and its effectiveness. The entire area of accountability establishes the basis on which to repeatedly ask that question whenever measurable accountability seems just out of reach or downright impossible. Once again, small gains in accountability can yield big gains in productivity and profits.

Transform the perception of values-driven discipline from punishment into performance improvement coaching. Take a tip from great dog trainers. When a dog misbehaves, they don't punish it. They correct the behavior and reward the dog when it performs correctly. Dogs love and respond to that. People respond in exactly the same way, except people are expected to get it right more quickly than dogs.

If you have ever participated in sports or in any other activity in which you had a coach, a teacher, or a director who used a disciplined approach to help you improve your skills and proficiency, I doubt you felt you were being punished. Unless the coach was a complete jerk. One of the things your coaches probably did was correct you as soon as you made a mistake, or exhibited bad form, or began to develop a bad habit. They did not wait a month or longer to review and critique your performance because, by that time, neither of you could accurately reconstruct what you did. And your coaches did not let small missteps slide by unaddressed. They understood that nuances mattered, and the only way to help you maximize your potential was to pay just as much attention to the smallest details as they did to major mistakes. And through it all, the harder your coaches were on you, the better you became. If you were smart, you were grateful.

One of my favorite and most effective techniques for using discipline as a performance improvement tool is this. When anyone exhibits behavior that does not align with your values, whether it's a single action or a pattern of conduct over some period of time, have a private one-on-one conversation with them. Describe the behavior. Then ask how that specific behavior demonstrates that they are living the particular value(s) you know they violated. Then be quiet. Let them try to explain; offer excuses; interpret their actions so as to demonstrate they were, in fact, living your value(s); describe mitigating factors that justify their conduct, etc. Allow them to continue, uninterrupted. They are in the process of burying themselves alive. Don't deny them the experience.

When they've finished, you can begin by pointing out that your values are unconditional; all the excuses and justifications in the world for not living them are irrelevant. Most of the time, you will not have to do that. In the course of offering up excuses, they will begin to see how their conduct was unacceptable. It's an eye-opener for them. Let them have a moment to feel it. From that place, your next series of questions revolve around what they could have and should have done instead. Now you have a course of action—one they have mostly created for themselves. So, they are more willing to take ownership of that course. You can end the discussion with a mutual agreement as to future actions and expectations. It is all about helping people improve their performance. I've used this approach hundreds of times. It's simple. It works. In fact, I can count on the fingers of one hand the number of times it hasn't.

Use peer influence. While peer *pressure* is no guarantee that certain people will fall in line, positive peer *influence* can be a strong motivator. There is one brain-driven reason why. It's because human beings want and need connection. It's a hardwired trait in all of us (certain types of severe mental disorders being the only exception). Once the majority of people in your organization demonstrate through their behavior they are living your values, the predominant energy shifts from rejecting to respecting. Talk to the thought leaders scattered throughout your organization. Help them see they are your cultural ambassadors of accountability. When any particular group within your company silently but civilly ostracizes people who do not live your values, one of three things will happen: those people will come around simply because they want to be accepted by their peers and feel a sense of belonging; they will voluntarily leave the company, opening the door to bring in new people who align with and live your values; or they will stay, aloof and unfulfilled. Sooner or later, their performance will fall below acceptable levels. You will know what to do at that point.

Lead by example. Hold yourself accountable to the same standards as everyone else. I addressed this in detail in the previous chapter with the story of my client, the president of his company, and how he held himself accountable in responding to a new employee's feeling of not being respected. The old adage applies here. *Become the change you want to create.*

These challenges can be daunting. Transforming your organization into a place where everyone is held to the same standard of measurable accountability is a continuous work in progress. The benefits of getting there are not an all-or-nothing game. Mastering Your Balance is an organic process in which everything affects everything else. You may never get to 100 percent accountability throughout your organization. Your successes may come at a glacial pace. But even incremental, measurable improvements in personal accountability can significantly help improve your performance and profits. The peripheral effects of any action can become a force multiplier and create a disproportional effect on the things they touch. This is clearly an area where you must have the attitude that even if you can't do it all, you should do everything in your power to achieve as much as possible.

There is an unarguable truth, borne out in countless experiences of companies whose fundamental business models and value propositions seem rock solid but who, at some point in their growth cycle, lost their cache. In the absence of individual accountability, the cultural norms that underpin brilliant execution become corrupted. As a result, the ability to execute and achieve strategic goals declines. Customers' experiences start to be less and less satisfying. Excellence is the exception, not the rule. Average becomes the new outstanding. The best performers find themselves working harder to achieve less. It's only a matter of time before their best days will be behind them. Then, they find reasons to leave. Some of the companies hang on for a while until they are acquired—usually for less than they were worth at their height. Some simply fail. They liquidate or file bankruptcy. A few go through a reorganization, with new leadership blood. And some of those companies do, in fact, experience a rebirth. Central to the success of a reorganization is the institution or restoration of individual accountability. How much pain and suffering could have been avoided if only that accountability was established and kept intact?

With the reality of so much disruptive change, it is difficult to see individual accountability as a root cause of organizational decline. Some would argue the root causes of those declines range from bad management and the wrong strategies to failure to adapt to disruptive innovations and customers' changing tastes or a host of other reasons, none of which are directly about being accountable. Those are all logical, measurable explanations/excuses for declines. They are all symptomatic. But after all the debates, one fundamental truth emerges. Values-driven leadership and the institution of individual accountability has never produced a negative outcome.

ACCOUNTABILITY AND TRUST

Finally, there is this. Every person, team, department, and company that is willing to make commitments and becomes measurably and individually accountable for meeting them, becomes more trustworthy. No one can order anyone to trust them. Trust can only be earned by becoming trustworthy. And trust precedes trade. Skepticism in the absence of experiencing results is also hardwired into our brains. It, too, is one of our instinctive survival mechanisms. Trust must pervade tribes and teams. Becoming and remaining trustworthy is an essential element in healthy cultures, and healthy cultures are essential to a healthy, balanced organization.

You can see how all the working parts continuously interact. They are the threads that, woven together, make up the fabric of every organization. Values-driven leadership is a prominently visible thread because its presence or absence has such an immediate and measurable impact on so much of what happens in both the daily life and long-term success of any company—including yours.

Over years of experience working with companies of all shapes and sizes and their leaders to develop our model of Mastering Your Balance, my partner, Jason Thompson, and I have come up with a list of the components of accountability that the highest performing companies and teams continuously strive to achieve. They are companies where values-driven leadership thrives, and measurable accountability is the cultural norm. It is a portrait of mastery.

- Everyone in the organization is held accountable for living your values.

- You always make specific individuals accountable, never an entire group/team or department. Accountability always attaches to a person and never to a system, process, or piece of equipment.

- You have formal procedures in place to positively acknowledge people when they go above and beyond the norm in the way they live your values and achieve extraordinary results—for the company and for themselves.

- You have systems and procedures in place to coach people when they slip up and fail to live your values. Coaching is not about punishment; it is about learning, improving performance, and growing.

- All your performance reviews include a section that evaluates every person as to how well they live your values. The results of those evaluations influence every person's compensation and their prospects for promotion and career advancement.

- When people fail to live your values, it always results in some measurable consequence—like performance improvement coaching, appropriate discipline, reductions in incentive compensation, demotions, and ultimately termination.

- You use your values in your recruiting, interviewing, hiring, and onboarding new employees. Candidates who do not or will not align with your values are not hired. That is true for all positions at every level in your company.

- Your values are aligned with your culture, strategies, and greater purpose. You make certain that is always the case.

- You consciously live your values. They are the core of helping you continuously improve. But you do not obsess about them. You do it, in large part, to prevent unhealthy mistakes, so you don't have to react after the damage has been done.

None of this is rocket science. You have probably seen many of these elements before. Their power comes from their collective presence. Achieving and maintaining universal accountability is and will always be a work in progress. As I've said before, it's not an all-or-nothing game; incremental improvements will move you toward Mastering Your Balance and yield measurable results.

The success of everything I've presented here rests on the level of your commitment and the excellence of your execution.

Now let's look at how it plays with your culture.

CHAPTER 7

Shape Your Culture

*Culture is the collective whole of what you do,
how you do it, and why you do it. It is shaped
and expressed by the values you live.*

That describes culture in its most fundamental context. If only it played out so simply in real life. Leaders of small companies serving local markets with a relatively small array of products that address a narrow set of needs can usually shape their cultures to behave and perform with one voice and deliver a consistent experience. Internally, they can more easily run as one unified team operating with a uniformly understood and executed set of behaviors because the relatively narrow scope of the business, diversity of thought, and need for creative experimentation—along with the people who bring it—lends itself to a unified culture.

At the other end of the cultural spectrum are large global companies. They operate in many countries, offer many products and/or services, sell to a variety of customers across many lines of business, and have thousands of employees. Cultural uniformity from country to country is impossible. Even if it was possible, it would not be a good thing. Every country has its own elements of cultural uniqueness.

"THE ROLE OF A CREATIVE LEADER IS NOT TO
HAVE ALL THE IDEAS; IT'S TO CREATE A CULTURE
WHERE EVERYONE CAN HAVE IDEAS AND FEEL THAT
THEY'RE VALUED."

—Ken Robinson

Between those two extremes lies everyone else. Companies with varying mixtures of products and services, making, selling, and distributing them in markets of all sizes to customers of all descriptions—and having a diverse range of cultural complexity. All cultures have unique characteristics.

Every organization's culture is the centerpiece for how and how well stuff gets done. And all companies of every size and level of complexity share certain common behavioral characteristics. Those universal characteristics that relate to the quality of Mastering Your Balance are the subject of this chapter. I will lay out what those characteristics are and what you can do to ensure they are expressed in ways that contribute to the health, productivity, and relevance of your culture. When you do that, you will have created a culture that contributes mightily to having a well-balanced organization.

Cultures are more complex than a single set of prevailing actions that define a norm. What you do, and how and why you do it, are things that have multiple interpretations as to how they play out experientially and stylistically in the multifaceted realm of reality. Personalities; politics (meaning multiple agendas); tribal vs. collaborative behavioral norms baked in by years of repetitive, unchallenged practices; laws and union contract requirements; conflicts created by multigenerational and multiethnic workforces, etc., all come together to create cultures sharing many characteristics, but each one has its own unique personality and style. Just like people. Because, of course, cultures are collections of people.

ELEMENTS OF A HIGH-FUNCTIONING CULTURE

The fundamental lesson is that the more focused leaders are, the clearer and more explicit your vision and values are, the more well-defined your strategic and tactical goals are, the more effectively your culture will perform. Explicitness and clarity are absolutely essential, as organizations become flatter and decision-making is driven further down into the operational ranks of any company. When you can formulate and communicate a clear vision and greater purpose (the why), clearly define needed outcomes (the what), and trust people at all levels of the organization to self-organize and execute most effectively to achieve those goals (the how), you will have the elements of a highly functioning culture in place.

Examples of shifts from stifling over-control to structures and cultures that enable more self-organization are:

- **Creating flatter organizations that drive decision-making down through the organization, closer to ground-level operations.** The quality and speed of decisions improve. More employees are integrally involved in developing and executing the tactics needed to achieve strategic goals. Morale, productivity, and results improve.

- **Increasing transparency.** Strict, traditional "need-to-know" criteria that leave employees largely in the dark is replaced by keeping people continuously informed about the big picture and giving them a proactive view of the things that directly and indirectly affect their work. The working mantra you can use to guide the level of transparency is: *If it involves me, involve me.* In doing that, you give people meaning. They know what they do contributes to a larger purpose. They are important, and what they do makes a difference. That is empowering.

- **Increasing diversity, which includes diversity of thought, age, race, sex, and cultural backgrounds.** Greater creativity, a broader view, and more informed beliefs about how society and markets work improve your ability to seize the opportunities and adapt to the challenges of an ever-changing world.

Now, let's get back to culture directly. I have said a number of times how important it is that all the elements of balance must align for you to operate and succeed at your highest level of potential. And you will hear that recurring theme throughout this book.

"THE POINT IS NOT TO BE IN CONTROL,
BUT TO BE IN TUNE."
—*Ed Moses*

The unique importance of your culture in this equation is this: All the elements of balance come together, transform from intention, and present themselves to the world in the form of behavior. *The ways in which all the people who comprise your culture behave, execute, and deliver experiences create the results that define your organization. Their outsized influence makes your culture the most visibly potent element in your company's being.*

That is why the things you do to create, guide, and influence your culture have a disproportionately significant impact on your overall results.

How do you create that ideal culture? What should it look and act like? Why must it change at all? What criteria should you evaluate to assess the need for any kind of cultural adaptation to more effectively address your future?

A STRUCTURAL GUIDE TO HEALTHY CULTURE CREATION

The following list is what I call a structural guide. It consists of seven areas that warrant your attention to help you create and sustain a healthy, high-performing culture:

▶ **Choose and live values that are right for you.**

- The only values that have a chance of working are those that align with who you truly are and what you're committed to be held accountable for living.

- Your values are designed to make you authentic, not popular. Nothing speaks more convincingly than your authentic self.

- Your values must align with the kind of culture you want to create, the people you want to attract, and the wants and needs of the customers you serve.

Anything less than that will create an undercurrent of dysfunction that will put unwanted limitations on your ability to reach your full potential.

- IBM offers a good example. It operates in 170 countries throughout the world. How could one set of values work in all those cultures? IBM settled on three core values, all customer-focused:

  - Dedication to every client's success.

  - Innovation that matters, for our company and for the world.

  - Trust and personal responsibility in all relationships.

Because all these values focus on the customer, IBM can transcend the cultural differences that exist in the many countries in which it operates. It allows the company to collaborate within its own organization without being conflicted by different cultural customs. It focuses on outcomes, defined by its customers' experiences, and the achievement of its own goals.

IBM's values go even further. They go beyond the traditional limits of being a set of beliefs defined by behavior. Its values have become the structural glue that binds and guides the workings of its organization. As they describe it, you cannot run an organization of more than 300,000 people in 170 countries with anything that looks like a conventional organization structure. It would be too unwieldy, too inefficient, and too slow to act. So, its values are not mere suggestions—they are the law, the structure, and the criteria by which the company governs itself. They define focus, shape strategies, and express the standards by which performance is measured. They underpin the culture and provide the criteria for the skills, personalities, and beliefs IBM uses to hire people. And those values are aligned with IBM's vision and purpose.

▶ **Embrace diversity of thought.**

- Replace immediate judgment (of other people's ideas, approaches, thought processes, perspective) with active curiosity.

- Whenever you feel yourself disagreeing or wanting to challenge, reject, or criticize—stop. Replace that urge with "tell me more" or "please elaborate."

- Enhance your curiosity with a desire to experiment, to experience something new.

- Whenever you are conflicted by the feeling that what you are being asked to consider or do is counterintuitive to what you have always believed to be right—stop and tell yourself you are in the right place. Conflict, both internal and external, is a prerequisite to change.

  - If you can do all those things—for yourself and for your people—you can achieve a masterful level of cultural adaptability.

▶ **Make people measurably accountable for living your values.**

- Accountability, to most people, equates to blame and punishment. Change that perception by handling it correctly.

- Holding people measurably accountable is about continuous performance improvement. It's a coach correcting an athlete's form and execution to get a better result. It's a film director yelling "cut" and working with the actors to deliver the message and tone needed to tell the story the way it needs to be told.

- When things go wrong, don't ask, "Whose fault is it?" or "Who is to blame?" Instead, ask, "Who is responsible?" The words fault and blame suggest someone needs to be punished. Responsibility suggests using the experience to learn, improve, and grow. Taking responsibility demands that you be accountable.

▶ **Have a pervasive practice of always making and keeping commitments—as opposed to expending best efforts and merely "trying."**

- Commitments demand specificity. Whenever and wherever they apply, there must be mutually agreeable dates, times, and descriptions of deliverables regarding what is being committed.

▶ **Constantly ask *what-would-it-take* questions whenever you encounter barriers that stand in the way of accomplishing** any goals you have set—no matter how big or small they might be.

The fundamental purposes of the question is to:

- Create a clean-sheet-of-paper context for thinking that strips away the self-limiting beliefs everyone has and constrains the possibilities of what you can achieve.

- Open the exploration of ambitious possibilities, and embrace possibilities that break from conventional wisdom and go beyond what has been deemed "practical."

- A major benefit of these kinds of *what-would-it-take* questions is that they invariably help you achieve more than you imagined; they help you raise your performance bar to a higher level.

▶ **Become transparent in the sense that your people are aware of, informed, and kept continuously in the loop as to whatever is happening in the organization that might directly or indirectly affect them.**

- Transparency makes it easier for people to trust their leaders and their leaders' actions. It stimulates engagement; people want to become involved when they know what's going on. It builds loyalty in the sense that people can connect what they do with how and why it and they are relevant, and that they make a difference.

- There are some organizations, or departments within organizations, where confidentiality is needed. In those instances, the goal of being transparent translates to having people know *there is no hidden agenda.* From that place, you can be seen as being trustworthy—and mutual trust is within your grasp.

- The opportunity for transparency can be seen in many areas at all levels of your operation. To illustrate, several years ago, I had a conversation with the CEO of a small manufacturer and distributor of nutritional supplements. In its business, confidentiality about product formulation was critical. So was confidentiality about financial results. Knowledge of its profits and cash flow could be used by competitors to gain competitive advantages and hurt its growth.

At the same time, the CEO was aware that her factory employees were going about their work in a methodical, uninspired way. Productivity was okay but not great. New ideas about process improvements were zero. Getting people to go the extra mile to fill emergency orders required a massive effort on the part of management.

Here is what she did. Once a month, as soon as the financial statements were prepared, the CEO and the CFO held a meeting with all the factory employees—at all levels—on the floor of the factory during an extended morning break. The two executives explained, in lay terms, what its monthly financial performance meant to the company; how it affected the company's ability to satisfy its customers; how it affected its ability to create new products; how it added funds (or not) to the quarterly bonus pool to be paid to all the factory workers; and how it helped them grow, add new jobs, afford wage increases to existing workers, and be seen as more important in its world. At the end of their presentation, they opened the floor to questions. And they answered every question candidly and authentically.

They also cautioned their employees that the information they were receiving was confidential, and they were receiving it because it was essential they knew the importance of what they were doing, and the effect their efforts had on creating great results. They were told the leaders believed in them, trusted them, and wanted them to know what they did was vital, and *they were important.*

Productivity improved within a few months—rapidly. Ideas to improve certain processes spewed forth. Nobody leaked any information—at least during the time I stayed in contact with the CEO (about a year).

The CEO's actions brought about a cultural change. Trust, engagement, resourcefulness, morale, reductions in turnover, fewer sick days taken, production efficiencies, and their associated cost reductions—all those things improved.

This may sound a bit like a fairy tale, but it happened. It happened because the CEO and her CFO were willing to ask themselves *what-would-it-take* questions about how to improve the operating results. They confronted their self-limiting beliefs about the nature of trust; they had to trust their people to receive and treat confidential financial information appropriately. That proved to be their tipping-point moment. It took them a few months of agonizing discussions to work up the courage before finally taking that leap of faith, followed by several sleepless nights of worry over being wrong about trusting their people. But it proved to be the right decision.

The leaders moved from dread to delight. They faced their fears. They embraced new possibilities and experienced unimagined results. Where are your opportunities to do the same in your company?

▶ **Strive to engage in win-win interactions—about everything. Override normal tribal instincts; replace them with inclusion and collaboration.**

Several years ago, I was working with one of the Big Four accounting and consulting firms. It was incurring an opportunity cost that defied common sense.

The firm's official mantra was: *Consulting is our future. Auditing is a commodity with intense competition and shrinking profit margins. Our tax practice is solid, but its growth rate is slow. We must look to our consulting practice to lead us to robust growth in revenue and profits.*

Those were the words. Reality was different. Tribal mistrust ruled. Audit partners were jealous over the larger fees and greater profits consulting engagements produced. And they feared if the consultants mishandled an engagement, the entire client relationship, including the auditing engagement, would be lost to a competitor.

Those were self-imposed fears. If anything, the opposite was true. Good outcomes generated by successful consulting engagements strengthened the overall client relationship and provided greater assurance of retaining auditing engagements without needing to reduce fees.

But fear ruled. When audit partners became aware of their clients' needs for consulting help, they referred those opportunities to other firms: competitors. Their logic was if the consulting engagement went poorly, their audit relationship would remain safe. That was a mind-boggling, embedded cultural practice.

What would it take to change their culture and replace those fears with truth, trust, and a change in behavior?

We put together a plan we called "take-an-auditor-to-lunch." A senior consulting principal would invite a senior audit partner to a working lunch meeting where the consulting principal would paint a picture of how a collaborative approach to client services opportunities, and a creative approach to fee allocation between the two groups, might forge a working partnership—one in which the auditing people would view the consultants as an asset and not a threat. The consulting principals also brought with them documented testimonials from happy clients.

The new fee-splitting portion appealed to the senior auditing partners.

But the reactions of the general population of auditing partners resembled a typical bell curve. A small percentage said *no way*. The majority showed an open-minded, curious interest but were too timid to be the first to do it. And a small percentage of thought leaders said, *let's try it*.

They began some engagements with the thought leaders. Word spread with the help of an orchestrated communication strategy. The open-minded-but-timid folks followed. It worked for them as well. The closed-minded audit partners remained out, perhaps too embarrassed to admit they could be wrong. It took the better part of two years to achieve the sufficient critical mass needed to represent a new cultural norm. But the change was measurable, and based on performance-driven results, hugely profitable.

Cultural change happened. Strategic goals, strategies, and tactics developed to achieve those goals became more collaborative (between the auditing and consulting groups) and more ambitious. And the changes in behavior helped everyone reflect on how they interpreted the meanings of some of their values as they pertained to how they best served their clients and how they interacted with each other.

And it all began by asking, "What would it take?"

This story illustrates several things. It shows the organic connection between the elements of balance—in this case, the degree to which values, culture, and strategy are intertwined— and how dysfunction in any one of them will negatively impact the others. The result will be felt in lower expectations and reduced performance. People will work harder and still operate below their full potential. And worse, no one will see it that way.

What did its clients see? Those clients were, for the most part, sophisticated organizations. They were most likely aware of the full range of services offered by all the Big Four firms. If I was a senior executive in one of those companies, I would ask myself, "Why, when my auditing firm knows full well all of the services it offers beyond auditing and tax work, would it recommend another firm to help us in the technology consulting area? It must really suck in that area. Good to know." And I might casually mention that to some of my executive friends over a couple of drinks after a round of golf.

It's obvious that cultures are complex, sometimes mysterious, misunderstood, often effective in certain areas and not so much in others. How they are allowed to lead to dysfunction is sometimes enabled by leaders' blind spots.

CULTURE CHANGE, COMPLEXITY, AND DYSFUNCTION

Of course, unless you are a new startup, you already have an established culture. If, based on the criteria listed above (or any other appropriate criteria), you determine certain changes are required, you must address two challenges. The first is abandoning existing habits that no longer serve you—getting out of your comfort zone. The second is learning new habits to replace those given up. Without acquiring a new habit to replace the old one, you will be operating in a vacuum. Vacuums are not sustainable. In time, you will revert to your old behaviors.

Disciplined repetition is the key skill needed to acquire any new habit. Mastering that skill reminds me of the old joke about the tourist visiting New York City for the first time. As he walks down a street in Manhattan, he stops a guy coming toward him and asks, *"How do I get to Carnegie Hall?"* The guy answers: *"Practice, practice, practice."*

Learning any new habit means that you will be awkward for a time. Your awkwardness will make you feel uncomfortable, incompetent, and perhaps incapable. You will make progress slowly. Then, one day, you will realize you are no longer uncomfortable. You will have arrived at a place I call skill neutral. You're not bad, but you're not yet good. You are, however, good enough and motivated enough to want to continue to learn and grow.

Growth adds complexity to cultures. That introduces a new challenge. Complexity can spawn subcultures. Competing agendas, differing views on the direction of the company, and a lack of confidence in leadership are but a small sampling of what can create *ideological silos* that operate as unaligned *cultures within a culture*. Sometimes, senior leadership is not even aware that these subcultures exist. This blindness might sound obvious, but I have seen the reactions of senior executives in large organizations when they became aware of their own subcultures. They were in shock at discovering their own blind spot to a reality even though all the signals of its existence were hiding in plain sight.

In its broadest context, when your culture is seamlessly aligned with all the elements of balance, they collectively enable you to perform at your highest potential. When they conflict, you endure some dysfunction. You work harder to achieve your goals. Success is more draining—financially, emotionally, and physically. In that state, scalability becomes a growth-limiting challenge. If you've been trapped in that state for some time, you see it as normal. It's life. You deal with it.

The reasons for dysfunction are many. The sheer complexity of your culture—there are lots of moving parts with frequently changing interactions between those parts—is one big reason. Here are some examples:

- The changing generational dynamic of workforces. Younger people have different attitudes about work and the intrinsic and extrinsic rewards they are looking for. Many younger people have a different sense of a work/life balance than the generation they are replacing.

- An evolving attitude and comfort level regarding the pace of adaptive change needed to keep a job. As a society, we need to become lifelong learners to remain employed and employable. Many people simply don't want to have to do that. Those who do and those who don't can create polarizing forces that divide cultures and make them dysfunctional.

- Conflicting attitudes about what constitutes great customer experiences. Those differences can prove divisive; threaten the performance of cultures; and cause significant harm to your brand, revenue, and earnings. The list goes on, but I think these examples illustrate the point.

Later in the book, I will present some case studies that illustrate the effects of the lack of alignment between multiple components of balance and how they were successfully addressed.

ELEMENTS OF A HEALTHY CULTURE

But first, I will conclude this chapter with a picture of the characteristics of a healthy, balanced culture, and how it seamlessly aligns with the other elements of balance.

- We actively recruit and hire a diverse group of people. By diverse, we mean things such as people with different perspectives and beliefs; different backgrounds; different life and work experiences; different races, religions, and cultures; different ages; etc.

- We encourage diverse views and ideas. When people express out-of-the-box opinions and ideas, they are heard, and their ideas are examined—not dismissed. This holds true in both formal processes and informal, casual conversations that occur in day-to-day interactions.

- Meetings are used to constructively resolve issues and develop opportunities. They are held when the purpose and subject cannot be communicated in other ways (like an email). Meeting agendas are published and distributed to attendees in advance. People show up on time and prepared. Meetings begin and end on time. When meetings produce actions to be taken, those actions are put in writing, and the appropriate people make commitments and assume responsibility and accountability for the intended results.

- When things go wrong (objectives not met, mistakes made, deadlines missed, etc.), leaders do not *blame* people but rather look at who is *responsible*. Blame suggests that someone must be punished. Responsibility suggests that someone is accountable and needs to take corrective action. Additional training/coaching might be required. Mistakes are seen as a platform to learn, get better, and grow.

- There is high value placed on creativity. There is a healthy tolerance for people making mistakes as part of their and the company's learning process. We are willing to think and act outside the box. Innovation is part of our growth.

- Our culture and the behaviors we adopt influence everything we do as individuals and as a company. Because of that, we make sure our culture aligns with our values, strategies, and greater purpose.

- If we see evidence a silo exists, we act to eliminate it. A silo is a group of people—a team, a department, or a store, etc.—that operates with its own set of rules. It becomes a separate culture. It has its own leaders and ways of doing things. It could have different goals. Silos exist in many companies. We believe they are usually unhealthy for the company as a whole. One exception might occur if a group or department needs to have its work be confidential.

- We understand the importance of making and keeping commitments (as opposed to merely trying). A *commitment* means: I will do this, and I will get it done when I said I would—no matter what. *Trying* means: I'll give it my best shot, but I can't guarantee I'll deliver. Keeping our commitments demonstrates integrity. Making and keeping our commitments says we are accountable. Simply trying leaves wiggle room and makes it difficult to hold anyone accountable.

- We believe "good enough is not good enough." Our performance bar is never set so low that we celebrate average performance as excellent.

- We support continuous learning—at all levels. Individual learning and development programs are available to everyone in our organization. Formal processes are in place for selecting deserving candidates and choosing the nature of the training along with the cost subsidies. Supporting continuous learning gives us a competitive advantage.

- Our culture is highly adaptive to the continuous changes occurring throughout our industry. We constantly challenge our cultural practices and change them when conditions so warrant. Nothing in our culture is set in stone. Disruptive change provides new opportunities for continued growth and long-term success.

- We strive to achieve transparency—to continuously let all our people know what our company is doing strategically, its progress and status regarding our objectives and KPIs, why everyone's work is important and relevant, how it impacts our success, and that they matter. We do this formally, with a defined process.

Let me emphasize one element that stands out. Diversity. When you embrace diversity of thought, ethnicity, religious beliefs, gender, and age—you enlarge your talent pool. An enlarged talent pool fosters greater creativity, which, in turn, creates more choices and makes you more adaptable. Adaptability makes you more resilient. When you are more adaptable, you can achieve greater growth and sustained relevance. This state of cultural health is equal parts wisdom, common sense, and the will to create it.

So why doesn't everyone just do it? Because diversity is at odds with our tribal instincts—the zero-sum, win-lose behaviors that are normal human nature. Diversity requires collaboration, trust, and a win-win approach in your interactions. It's upsetting to have your beliefs about what is good, right, and traditional called into question. Yet, creating a healthy, vibrant culture is the linchpin of Mastering Your Balance. It is the centerpiece of your ability to scale your growth and maximize your potential. Your culture will always be in a fluid state, a continuous work in progress, needing to constantly gauge the winds of change. You will forever need to assess the perceived strengths of tradition against the possibility that you are practicing outmoded, counterproductive rituals that have lost their relevance and stymie your growth.

Your culture does not just exist in an internal bubble. It communicates to your world. It is a place where your self-perceptions collide with the inconsistencies of how the rest of the world sees you. Coming to grips with those conflicting perceptions demands introspection. I will explore that in a later chapter.

But now, let's look at the next element of Mastering Your Balance: strategy.

CHAPTER 8

Align Your Strategies

Strategies put legs on your vision and create links to your greater purpose. But no matter how intelligent your strategies might be, in the absence of brilliant execution, the best you will achieve is mediocrity. And if your strategies are not aligned with your culture and you work extra hard, you could also achieve burnout.

Viewed through a positive lens, the right strategies, executed with brilliance, represent the measurable means to stand out, to separate yourself from the herd, and to maximize your tangible value in the world.

Strategies are the most quantifiable performance element in a balanced organization. To start, they must be conceived and solidified by the right tactics, human and capital resources, assignment of responsibilities, and time frames needed to execute them. With those steps completed, they become the place where the product of creation must be aligned with your vision and greater purpose, merged with the behaviors of being (values and culture) and the skill of doing (execution). The obvious conclusion of all this is that having a masterfully balanced organization gives you the greatest potential to conceive strategies more boldly and execute more brilliantly.

"STRATEGY IS A COMMODITY; EXECUTION IS AN ART."
—*Peter Drucker*

In a perfect world, developing and executing strategies and achieving the goals they describe would be a relatively simple and straightforward process. In that perfect world, there would be universal understandings as to exactly what strategy means, how tactics support strategies, how to assign resources to execute them, how progress is measured, and how individual accountability is established and applied. In addition, the ideal number of strategic objectives being pursued at any given time would be universally agreed upon throughout the business world.

Unfortunately, we don't live in a perfect world. Here are a few examples.

STRATEGY UPS AND DOWNS

One former client described its strategy this way. Every morning, we get up and go sell something, our production people produce it, and our distribution arm delivers it. We look for opportunities and exploit them. We deal with problems and solve them. At the end of the day, if we've done it well, we make a decent profit. We've been doing it that way for over twenty-five years. Seems to be working out just fine. It sounds like a successful small company, doesn't it? Wrong. It was a company with annual sales of over $2 billion, doing business throughout the US. It was opportunistic yet crisis-oriented. As a result, it was resistant to making proactive investments with long-term potential. If it didn't see an immediate return, it held back. Still, it was highly profitable—until disruptive changes in its industry left it unable to adjust. It went badly for the company. It blamed conditions beyond its control. After a number of reactive, strategic scrambles to right the ship, it filed for Chapter 11 bankruptcy.

Another former client was drowning in strategic planning overthink. It had nineteen strategic objectives and business case analyses for each one, all of them carefully set forth with a staggering number of tactics, human and capital resources allocated and budgeted, meticulously detailed progress reports, and pretty charts depicting performance against goals. It used that approach for five consecutive years—and did not achieve a single major objective.

But its CEO was committed to changing that experience. We helped the company develop an execution-focused strategic plan with three key strategic objectives, the optimum number of tactics needed to execute, a game plan for dealing with the known challenges, specific accountabilities for results, and a timeline for completion. The strategies aligned with its vision, values, and culture. In the beginning, many of its senior executives resisted. But they agreed to do it anyway. In the first year, the company achieved all of its objectives and increased its profit by 42 percent over the previous year.

A Big Four accounting and consulting company I worked with had an interesting approach to strategy. Senior leaders handed down an edict to all the practice management partners and principals throughout the firm. "Grow your practice revenue and earnings by 20 percent in the coming year." The details were as follows. "You are smart. You know your market. You know your people. You know what skill sets and subject matter expertise you need. You know what support resources you have for administration, training, and logistical support. Figure it out. And you *will* be held accountable." And, for the most part, the practice partners delivered. They also experienced some unwanted side effects: a high burnout rate experienced by many employees (partners and non-partners alike), breakdowns in cross-practice communication and collaboration (everyone was too singularly focused on their personal goals to care about their colleagues), and the unmeasured opportunity cost caused by failures to cross-sell services because of their ineffective collaboration. But on the surface, hey, the company grew by 20 percent. What it did not see was that, if it had a more balanced organization, it could have achieved much greater growth and less burnout—with no greater (and perhaps less) effort. I'd love to claim credit for helping it see the light and improve. But that was not part of my engagement; the firm was doing well enough, and no one in leadership saw the need to entertain that possibility. They chose to see "good" as "great."

To put the icing on the cake, numerous articles have been published over several years stating that senior leaders in many large companies believe their strategic objectives are, in and of themselves, their strategies. I suspect that misconception is not confined to leaders of large organizations.

For clarity, let me set forth a foundation for defining what constitutes a strategy in any size organization.

STRATEGY DEFINED

A strategy is a plan of action, underpinned by an appropriate set of tactics, designed to achieve a given strategic objective. The plan should set forth the following:

- The tactics you intend to use

- The needed human and capital resources

- Individual responsibility(s) for achieving the goal(s)

- The milestones by which you will measure progress

- The barriers and challenges you expect to encounter and plans for dealing with them

- The time frame(s) needed to achieve your objective

- A description of what success looks like

Underneath that high-level definition, there are a broad spectrum of actions taken by organizations to make it work. Some companies create a formal set of detailed steps that support the value of the strategy. A formal business case justification might include elements such as analyses of market factors that support the strategy, a competitive analysis to support the wisdom of the strategy, estimated return on investment (ROI), justification for the allocation of resources (compared to alternative uses of human and financial capital), and more. Some organizations don't provide that depth of analysis; they just stick to the essential elements related to execution.

Here is where Mastering Your Balance comes into play. All the elements of strategy creation, justification, development of the tactics needed for execution, and allocation of resources— all leading up to action—should also undergo an additional, rigorous examination to make certain the strategy and the tactics that drive execution align with the other elements of balance.

Why?

Because trying to execute a strategy that is not aligned with your vision, values, culture, and greater purpose is like staging a play in which the script is written but some of the individual actors' roles are not. The actors' performances will never fully connect to the story. It will never be smooth, well told, or fully understood. It will be filled with conflicts. And the audience will leave with perhaps an appreciation for the play's intention, but the overall performance will leave them unsatisfied.

To more graphically illustrate the costly effects of disconnection, I will bring back my favorite poster child of dysfunction, cited as an example in some earlier chapters of this book: Wells Fargo. In its case, we need to look no further than its vision and values—and its seemingly callous disregard for them in the course of the tactics it used to execute one of its strategies.

Wells Fargo's vision once again:

> *We want to satisfy our customers' financial needs and help them succeed financially. This unites us around a simple premise. Customers can be better served when they have a relationship with a trusted provider that knows them well, provides reliable guidance, and can serve their full range of financial needs.*

Wells Fargo's values:

- **What's right for customers.** We place customers at the center of everything we do. We want to exceed customer expectations and build relationships that last a lifetime.

- **People as a competitive advantage.** We strive to attract, develop, motivate, and retain the best team members—and collaborate across businesses and functions to serve customers.

- **Ethics.** We're committed to the highest standards of integrity, transparency, and principled performance. We do the right thing in the right way and hold ourselves accountable.

- **Diversity and inclusion.** We value and promote diversity and inclusion in all aspects of business and at all levels. Success comes from inviting and incorporating diverse perspectives.

- **Leadership.** We're all called to be leaders. We want everyone to lead themselves, lead the team, and lead the business—in service to customers, communities, team members, and shareholders.

One of Wells Fargo's strategies:

- **Aggressively cross-sell a variety of its retail products and services to existing customers.** This would increase revenue and strengthen the depth and scope of existing customer relationships, thereby creating more value for customers and greater insulation from competitors. Sounds good.

- **Tactical execution**—a.k.a. where the shit hits the fan

  – Mobilize about 5,000 mid- and lower-level employees in the Retail Division with little training or knowledge regarding the products they would be selling. Do not attempt to provide training prior to launching the initiative.

— Give them ambitious sales goals that far outstrip their abilities to achieve those goals (without further training). Use fear and threats of termination as the primary motivators to spur sales.

— Tacitly inform those employees to use "any means necessary" to achieve their goals.

— Do not question or audit the improving sales results to make certain those sales were made properly and the customers who "purchased" the products did so willingly and were properly informed as to what they were buying.

— Turn a blind eye to the fact that employees are creating new accounts and issuing credit cards to existing customers without their knowledge and approval. The numbers look good—that's what matters. No one has noticed. Life is good.

I cannot know or speculate as to the thinking, motivations, and true intentions of the leaders at Wells Fargo who orchestrated and executed the tactics that were employed. But it is glaringly apparent they disregarded their stated values. And they chose a path that took them far off the course set forth in their vision.

A critical point in this story was that Wells Fargo's vision and values were all crafted, published, and proclaimed as its promise to the world *before* it engaged in the conduct that wreaked financial and cultural havoc on the company. One can only ask, "Where were the leaders who could have stepped up and stopped this debacle long before it reached the monstrous magnitude of mismanagement that we have all seen play out on a public stage?"

The gross nature of it all makes it easy for me to use them as an overarching example of everything that can go wrong when all the elements of balance are not aligned. I guess I should thank them for that. It made writing this part of the book so much easier.

THE POWER OF CONNECTION

Vision

When there is a clear connection between any given strategy and achieving the strategic goal(s) it defines, it gives people a solid understanding as to the wisdom of that strategy, and people (your culture) are much more focused. There is no conflict, confusion, or hesitancy—conscious or subconscious—that can diminish the collective energy and commitment to achieving your strategic objective.

If you are crafting a strategy you know conflicts with your vision, tell your people and tell them why. It's not ideal to develop those kinds of strategies, but if you believe you have a good reason, and it is truly an exception and not the norm, the worst thing you could do is try to hide it. Tell the truth, get in front of the story. Because if you don't, you risk diminishing your credibility in more areas than those directly affected by your wayward strategy.

Values And Values-Driven Leadership

When your strategies align with your values, and people are held measurably accountable for living those values, executing your strategies eliminates behavioral or ethical conflicts. It sharpens people's focus. On the other hand, a situation in which people are being asked to do things that conflict with the company's values creates the kind of negative stress that distracts them, saps their energy, and slows them down.

Being measurably accountable for living your values easily translates into being measurably accountable for executing the tactics needed to achieve your strategic goals. When you establish that level of accountability, you will have paved the way to creating a culture of making and keeping commitments. That will replace the more toothless practice of attempting to hold people accountable for simply *trying*. Cultures of *commitment* can always set the performance bar higher than those that simply focus on *trying*.

Commitment fosters aspirational performance. Trying offers excuses for failure.

Culture

When you are able to set your performance bar higher, other things change. Oftentimes, new skills are needed. People are challenged to learn those skills and grow in the process. Your environment becomes more exciting. Creative ideas spring up where before, mindless habits formed from traditional practices produced acceptable but less than stellar results. It's a process, however, not an epiphany. This ain't the movies. Be patient. It will bubble up—from bottom to top.

Setting and achieving loftier goals changes people's perspectives about what is possible. They see the world and their place in it differently. Aspiration becomes inspiration. Self-limiting beliefs can be examined and discarded, replaced by a new set of cultural norms that make you more relevant, more valuable to the markets and customers you serve. Old traditions can be examined. You'll be better able to decide whether certain of your timeworn behaviors are a source of strength or a prison of counterproductive practices.

Aligning your strategies with your cultural capabilities is simply common sense in action. It's easy to see through the lens of hindsight the inevitable consequences of not doing that. It's a head-scratching moment for the spectators and critics—many of whom are customers, suppliers, bankers, and shareholders/investors—to witness the seemingly obvious ineptitude of leaders who fail to achieve that connection. Failure to align the two is one of the most easily preventable self-inflicted wounds of all. And yet—we see that failure time and time again.

Companies that employ a growth strategy that includes acquiring other companies seem particularly plagued by this cultural alignment blindness. Too many acquisitions are largely numbers-driven; cultural compatibility is assumed into existence, either at the time of closure or within a reasonable period of time thereafter.

We can see a monstrous failure to align strategy with culture, played out in the arena of organic growth with my poster child for bad behavior: Wells Fargo. In addition to what I cited earlier regarding conflicts with Wells Fargo's vision and values, its tactics to aggressively engage in cross-selling products to existing customers failed to recognize some basic cultural limitations: a woefully undertrained staff incapable of achieving impossible goals created by seemingly subjective wish lists. Rather than recognizing its error and course-correcting through additional training and resetting of its goals, it doubled down on irrationality, perhaps driven by unrealistic needs to increase shareholder (and executive) wealth. It was doomed from the start.

Greater Purpose

Whereas the alignment of your strategies with your vision helps establish your path to your legacy of *what* you commit to being, the alignment of your strategies with your greater purpose clearly establishes *why* you are doing it. Why gives life purpose, meaning, and relevance. Why makes people eager to get up and show up with all they have to give—mind, body, and soul.

When those things exist, a sense of commitment follows. You will have positioned yourself to set and achieve more ambitious goals.

THE POWER OF THREE

You can often inspire people by simply helping them discard their self-limiting beliefs about how things are, and paint a picture of new possibilities.

When you execute well, your success encourages your team. You already know that. But knowing it and mastering it are two different things. While many do well, only a few achieve mastery. But how *do* you get to mastery? You're already working your ass off. So, effort alone won't assure you get there.

Great strategies have these three fundamental characteristics:

- They are **Ambitious.** They take you beyond the boundaries of your self-limiting beliefs about what is possible. When appropriate, they are not afraid to take you beyond what is practical. When your assessment of possibilities uncovers exciting opportunities, your strategies should focus on quantum rather than incremental goals, your potential versus your self-limiting beliefs.

- They are **Creative.** They address doing/achieving new things. Or they have you doing old things in new ways. They do not allow you to fall into the trap of dismissing potentially lucrative opportunities by offering up the lazy rejection of "we tried that before; it didn't work."

- They are **Executable.** This one is the most important. Your ability to execute is the foundation of a solid strategy. It is a place from which you can create the tactical actions that align your ability to execute with the human and capital resources you either have or can acquire. Achieving a level of brilliant execution can only be accomplished when your strategies are aligned with your culture. Cultures only perform at their best when they are commitment-driven. Being commitment-driven requires that people accept responsibility for results and are willing to be personally accountable. Brilliant execution defines you. Anything less is just conversation.

Here is an illustrative story. Several years ago, I was working with a pilot group of independently owned dealers representing a large, multinational document management and fax machine manufacturer. Their industry was growing at an annual rate of 5 percent. They were closing only 25 percent of their sales opportunities when they were one of the finalists chosen to do a formal presentation. The dealers knew their closing rate needed to be closer to 50 percent to achieve their growth goals. Their salespeople were frustrated. They knew and believed in their products, and they presented well. Their prices were competitive, and their after-sales service was outstanding. What could the problem be?

Company executives believed it was a matter of chemistry between the competing sales reps and the potential clients' buyers. They reasoned they might need to generate more leads, but that would require hiring more sales reps. Perhaps they could invest in more sales training to improve their presentation skills. There were no easy answers, and every approach they considered meant doing more of what was not working.

I suggested a different approach. I suggested they create a presentation team of two people: the sales representative responsible for the account and a member of the after-sales tech/service team. We would create a sales presentation that would feel like an interactive stage play, with specific roles for the sales rep and the tech person.

The dealers told me: a) I did not fully understand how their business worked; b) I should know their tech people could not sell and did not want to sell; and c) even if they would be willing to try (which of course, they wouldn't), they had no presentation skills.

But the dealers were still willing to listen for a more detailed explanation. Credit to them.

I first reviewed what everyone already knew—just to put us all on the same page. To be chosen to make a presentation, their product was recognized as a possible selection by the potential client. Usually there were three finalists, occasionally four. All the products performed more or less equally. Everyone's price was within a whisker of the others. All of them professed to offer outstanding after-sales service. The common belief was that, at this point, it became a matter of chemistry. Superior charisma would win the day—unless some other secret sauce was introduced into the presentation. But what?

I presented this line of reasoning. The potential customer knew there was no essential difference between any of the products, and the prices would be virtually identical. The differentiator in the clients' minds was *not* charisma. It was about being convinced it would be buying a superior service experience, and it would have the fewest down days and hours over the course of a year. Having the tech support person there to graphically explain that experience could win the day. Salespeople, in situations like this, usually tended to oversell performance and service, but the clients knew when it came to service, the tech person represented the most credible source they could talk to. Tech people did not oversell; they told it like it was. They were far more credible. And with a properly structured presentation, the tech person would play the starring role in this one-act drama.

But the tech people would not want to do this, the executives said. This is not what they were trained to do. It's not what they like to do. They'd be terrible at it. But they agreed to ask the techies—just to appease me. With the first dealer in the group, we asked six technicians if they'd be interested in participating. Four of them said absolutely yes. We picked the two we felt had the most aptitude and would need the least training.

The salespeople would not like it, the executives said. They all wanted to be the star of the show when it got to the presentations. So, we asked the salespeople. Their response was unanimous. If you think this will increase our closing rate, then hell yes, we'll try it.

We began the test with one dealer and one team. We scripted the presentation, including all the guided Q&A focused on preventive and remedial maintenance. We rehearsed and rehearsed and rehearsed some more. We made the handoffs between the sales rep and the techie flawless and natural. Results were more than encouraging.

Fast forward six months. Closing rates went from 25 percent to 70+ percent. Revenue increased by 20 percent. No additional advertising expenses. No new sales personnel hired. Morale soared.

While I was not an employee with a diverse perspective, I was a credible outsider. The executives, to their credit, resisted but did not reject this new idea. They were willing to explore it.

More significantly, they were willing to abandon their self-limiting beliefs about why it could not be done. And they were willing to try. The results spoke for themselves.

The dealers overcame the behavioral gravitational pull of their cultural norms. It can be initially exhausting to overcome that pull in the course of attempting to execute a strategy that requires an ad hoc change in your cultural behavior, but the story of these dealers makes a strong case for instilling that discipline into your culture—of listening, erasing your self-limiting beliefs, and being willing to try new ideas.

The idea of having a creative culture does not adhere to a one-approach-fits-all description. It can be something as simple as exhibiting a willingness to listen to new ideas with an open mind and fully examine how you might put them to use—even if, and perhaps especially if, they contradict some historic cultural norms that might be obsolete. It can be an all-out focus on a complete reinvention of yourself, with all the attendant allocation of time and resources needed to do that. Or it can be anything between the two, based on your assessment of where you currently stand and where you want to be, in terms of your growth goals, competitive position, and available resources.

But one thing is absolutely true for everyone: doing nothing is not your best option.

YOUR STRATEGY REALITY

The following characteristics put into context how strategies are formulated and executed in a healthy, balanced organization. You can use this list as a tool to assess your current state of reality.

- When we formulate strategies, care is taken to make certain that they are always aligned with our vision, values, culture, and greater purpose. Anything less than full alignment will make it more difficult and more costly to achieve desired objectives. In some cases, it might be impossible.

- Once a strategy is formulated, the people who are primarily responsible and accountable for achieving the goals are named and appropriately assigned.

- When a formal analysis for obtaining approval of strategic objectives is prepared, it includes a section that demonstrates the alignment between the strategy and our values, and between the strategy and the cultural behaviors needed to achieve our objectives.

- There are always three strategic objectives being executed at any given time. No more, no less. When goals for a given strategy are achieved, or when the strategy is abandoned, a new strategic objective is put in its place.

- We have a formal understanding of how teams execute initiatives. Our approach is designed to ensure clarity regarding scope, needed resources, expected outcomes, and responsibilities. We consistently debrief to analyze our effectiveness, areas for improvement, and a focus on continuous improvement.

The critical piece in all of this is that these things are done as your strategies are being developed and hatched—and not after you reflected on the costs you incurred because you forgot them and somehow went off the rails. Having these elements in place will not, in and of themselves, guarantee you will execute your strategies brilliantly. These pieces, however, will put you in the best possible position to achieve your strategic goals in the most cost-effective and timely manner. Additionally, they will enable you to set more ambitious goals, reach higher, and challenge yourself in ways you may not have imagined were possible.

Let us now move to the final element of Mastering Your Balance: your greater purpose.

CHAPTER 9

Discover Your Greater Purpose

*Material wealth may allow you to go to sleep
in luxurious comfort, but greater purpose will
inspire you to leap out of bed in the morning.*

P ursuing a purpose greater than accumulating "stuff"
defines the difference between living and existing.
Material net worth is not more fulfilling than human
net worth.

"THE TWO MOST IMPORTANT DAYS IN LIFE ARE THE
DAY YOU WERE BORN AND THE DAY YOU DISCOVER
THE REASON WHY."

—Anonymous

Inspiring words to live by, perhaps. But how does greater
purpose contribute to Mastering Your Balance?

The answer takes us on a circular path. Ask yourself these
questions. Beyond making money, why are you here? How
will you leave this world somehow better for your presence?
What do you do that enriches the human experience? And how
will those things enhance your company's performance, help
you grow, and increase your material wealth? In other words,

how does greater purpose assist financial purpose and vice versa? More than that, how do the two become so seamlessly intertwined that pursuing either one automatically advances the other, at least in the long term?

The answer is, it depends. Answering those questions requires some context. Here are two examples of companies that have published their greater purpose:

- **Starbucks's** greater purpose: To inspire and nurture the human spirit, one person, one cup, and one community at a time

  This purpose suggests a global reach and a local presence. A Starbucks store becomes a gathering place for experiences. Students working on projects—alone or in small groups. Writers writing. Graphic artists designing. Business people meeting—for casual conversations or to discuss world-changing deals. First dates leading to romance or rejection. Or just a time out—a welcome respite from stress.

  All of these reasons for seeing Starbucks as the place with the ambiance to make them occur involve the Starbucks people creating the human interaction and the *cup of coffee and more* to complete the experience. And to make people think first (and hopefully only) about Starbucks being the *place* with tastes, smells, flavors, and a rich enough variety of yummy stuff to satisfy the thirst and hunger pangs in just the right amounts.

Formulate the right strategies; create and nurture the right culture; hire, train, and coach the right people to live the right values; and execute brilliantly to witness purpose and profits seamlessly glide into a place of market leadership—if not domination.

It all sounds noble. And it is. It's also practical, executable, and profitable—and it has created enormous shareholder wealth for Starbucks over more than twenty years. That is not just because the words are skillfully put together. It works because the intent of those words, put into action to direct an ever-growing body of human and capital resources is organized, aligned, and focused with all six elements of a balanced organization operating at exceptional performance levels. In the case of a growing organization with ambitious goals, greater purpose plays a major role in making the business model scalable. Without the presence of a greater purpose, it's impossible to achieve and sustain that level of success.

- **Patagonia** is a company that sells outdoor gear used in a variety of outdoor sports. Here is a quote from its website that describes its greater purpose:

  Our Reason for Being: *Patagonia grew out of a small company that made tools for climbers. Alpinism remains at the heart of a worldwide business that still makes clothes for climbing—as well as for skiing, snowboarding, surfing, fly fishing, paddling and trail running. These are all silent sports. None require a motor; none deliver the cheers of a crowd. In each sport, reward comes in the form of hard-won grace and moments of connection between us and nature.*

Our values reflect those of a business started by a band of climbers and surfers, and the minimalist style they promoted. The approach we take towards product design demonstrates a bias for simplicity and utility.

For us at Patagonia, a love of wild and beautiful places demands participation in the fight to save them, and to help reverse the steep decline in the overall environmental health of our planet. We donate our time, services and at least 1 percent of our sales to hundreds of grassroots environmental groups all over the world who work to help reverse the tide.

Patagonia is privately held. Its annual sales in 2015 were estimated at $750 million. Yvon Chouinard, its CEO and sole shareholder, has a net worth of $1 billion. Can greater purpose march side-by-side with financial wealth? Sure seems like it.

These examples have been about large companies with big visions (although Patagonia had a very modest beginning) and world-changing greater purposes. What about companies with more modest ambitions?

SCALING YOUR GREATER PURPOSE

Every element of Mastering Your Balance is scalable—including your greater purpose.

When you have a purpose beyond material wealth, creativity has a different sense of itself. It is broader in scope. Ideas outside the box of rigid conformity and mindless tradition flow more easily and your culture embraces and more readily explores those ideas.

In the long-term, any organization that has a purpose beyond building wealth or wielding power is more resilient and stronger than one without a greater purpose.

The irony here is that organizations that have a purpose beyond money or power will, in all likelihood, create more wealth for their owners than those that don't have that greater purpose. Making a positive difference in the world, serving a need, solving a problem, or creating new opportunities—making the world a better place for your having been here—make an organization more enduring and more profitable. Those that don't? They come and go, and they're not terribly missed. Who, besides its shareholders, employees, and creditors, was really saddened by the disappearance of Enron?

How will you make a difference in the world beyond building shareholder wealth? What are the greater implications of and the results realized by the people who use your products and services?

How do the differences you make factor into your strategic discussions and decisions? Are you prepared to say no to opportunities that contradict your reason for being? Are you willing to avoid hiring people who have conflicting beliefs and agendas that could undermine your greater purpose? Do you even consider those possibilities when you recruit and hire talent?

Suppose you are leading or are employed by a company whose only purpose is to generate a significant income for its owner(s), build their net worth, and enable them to sell the company and comfortably retire when they're ready. That's it. No purpose beyond that.

If your primary reason for being is purely to increase your personal wealth, succession planning is typically more challenging. Existing only for money, while having appeal for some, is not an inspiring reason for many people to want to build a long-term career with your organization.

Consider this idea: Define your greater purpose around creating a company whose purpose is to generate income and a comfortable retirement for the owner(s), *and* do it in such a way as to create long-term relevance and sustainability that will endure for generations to come.

That will require you to create a culture of people who embrace the kinds of diversity of thought leading to long-term strength. You will need to develop and execute strategies that are bolder and more profitable than perhaps the safer approaches taken by most companies that simply want to hang on to what they already have and avoid any level of risk (even though history is replete with stories that tell us that taking no risk is often the greatest risk). It means you will have to thoughtfully choose to live a set of values that align with the cultural norms and strategies you will need. In short, you will need to strive to operate at your highest potential—and achieve the level of balance necessary to do that.

If you do all that, you will improve your chances to maximize both your earnings and the fair market value of your business (your net worth). The continuing value of your company—after you retire—will have your employees looking at a future for themselves that makes being with you for the long term a good investment.

What would it take for you to envision and pursue a purpose beyond personal wealth? How would you approach people in your organization to participate in what that might look like? What is your appetite for that kind of refocus?

HOW GREATER PURPOSE FITS IN

Here is a set of criteria describing an organization with a greater purpose that reflects the importance of that purpose and how it aligns with the other elements of balance.

- We know profit is only the fuel that allows us to harness and focus our capabilities to make something beyond profit: impact.

- Our recruiting and hiring process includes communicating our greater purpose to all prospective employees. We seek people who identify with our purpose and are committed to do their part to help achieve it. If we identify a job applicant who is otherwise qualified but does not agree with our greater purpose, we usually do not hire that person.

- We actively encourage our employees to support organizations that align with our greater purpose. That typically involves an employee's participation in events and activities for those organizations. We usually contribute financially or allow our employees to spend a reasonable amount of paid time to participate (or both).

- We, as an organization, actively sponsor and support organizations, causes, and events whose activities align with our greater purpose.

- We make certain our greater purpose is a conscious element in crafting our strategic objectives and in making the business case for all our strategic and operational initiatives.

You have now seen all six elements of a balanced organization. How do you put all of this into play? How do you begin the next chapter of your journey—going from acceptable to exceptional? Let's look at that next.

CHAPTER 10

Now Make It Happen

You have now been introduced to all the elements of balance and have been shown how they can align and integrate to enable you to operate at your full potential.

Of course, the potential value of that information depends on how, how much, and how well you put it into play and execute.

> "THE PURPOSE OF LIFE IS TO CONTRIBUTE IN SOME
> WAY TO MAKING THINGS BETTER."
> —*Robert F. Kennedy*

The elements of balance already exist in your organization. They have affected your focus, structure, and performance for as long as your company has been in business. The state of your current reality is the result of how all of it came together through your decisions and behaviors up to this point. Hopefully, you have done well. However, as well as you've done, you still have untapped potential to be explored, developed, and rewarded. You are in a position to rise from acceptable to exceptional.

And what you've read can be the foundational guide to help you get there.

Here's how.

Begin with your assessment of how well your organization performs relative to its alignment with the elements of balance at their full potential. It's imperative to put a *you-are-here* dot on your map of reality. And if you are not perfectly aligned (and no one ever is), at what level of performance are you performing in comparison to the ideal—to your full potential? There is always an opportunity to do more, be more, and achieve greater heights. Developing a plan to Master Your Balance will help take you there.

When you have assessed your current status, some areas will jump out at you. They will shout, *"Look at me. Work on me first."* Those areas can be centered in any given element or in several connected ones. For example, certain strategy and culture issues might have some closely related needs/opportunities that would suggest you work on both of them at the same time. Or you might conclude you would benefit by creating greater clarity in some elements. I have seen many companies whose values are not spelled out in writing—and they should be.

Here's my advice. Begin anywhere you choose. There is no official starting point. The Mastering Your Balance model is circular and organic. All the elements will connect and interact, no matter where you focus. More importantly, executing is not an all-or-nothing proposition. Every single thing you do will have an impact on your overall performance. So, if you do even a little, you will see measurable benefits, often disproportionally greater than you might expect. If you do more, your results will become a force multiplier to encourage more still. You can set a variable pace for execution based on how your priorities and resources will shift over time. The important thing is to maintain some level of engagement at all times, so people keep your long-term goals top-of-mind, even when your focus is situationally short term.

My recommended methodology is simple. Always ask many, many *what-would-it-take* questions. About virtually everything. For example:

- *What would it take* to do a self-assessment of our level of performance compared to the ideals of a balanced organization? And if we can't do a sufficiently valuable self-assessment, what would it take to find other means by which we can assess our current state?

- *What would it take* for us to effectively hold everyone in our organization measurably accountable for living our values?

- *What would it take* to truly create a more culturally and creatively diverse culture so we can more effectively thrive in a changing world?

- *What would it take* to always begin and end our meetings on time?

The opportunities to ask *what-would-it-take* questions are virtually limitless. Your commitment to doing so should be as well.

Keep in mind that a primary purpose of the *what-would-it-take* question is to move your ego out of the room, thereby creating a clean sheet of paper devoid of your self-limiting beliefs and confirmation biases. You become free to be creative.

Here are a few areas for you to reflect on to help you focus on where you can realize the best return on investment in propelling your organization to achieve your full potential:

- **Good enough**—Where have we allowed "good enough" to be our performance benchmark? Why? What excuses have we made?

- **Self-limiting**—What self-limiting beliefs about certain areas of performance have we justified under the banner of "we need to be practical here"?

- **Out of the box**—What is our tolerance for embracing out-of-the-box thinking that challenges our present way of doing things—from small, everyday processes to the very core elements of our business model?

- **Diversity**—How much diversity of thought exists in our culture? Why isn't there more?

- **Creativity**—Is our definition of creativity confined to finding better ways to continue doing what we presently do? If so, why? Are we willing to incur the costs of experimenting (and failing) necessary to truly embrace the creative process—and the people whose creative passions we need?

- **Adaptability**—How adaptable is our culture to the disruptive changes that will be necessary to thrive through the pandemic and beyond?

Because all of us have some level of confirmation bias, and because our brains are wired to accept life as it has been presented to us, we all have self-limiting beliefs. Self-limiting beliefs are born out of fear—of something. And while fear can and often does propel us to change, the goal of fear-driven change is survival. On the other hand, a desire to change and grow that is based on achieving your full potential will almost always drive you to new and previously unimagined levels of performance. None of us continuously performs and achieves at our full potential. Which gives rise to the reality that:

You and everyone in your organization are more than you think you are. Use that reality to continuously propel you. To help you do that, here is the mantra we use at Axíes Group as our guide:

To achieve the improbable, you must first envision the impossible.

The only thing standing between you and the path forward is your willingness to take the first step. *So, what would it take for you to begin?*

If you've read this whole book, you are ready to begin. If you've read only the parts you think pertain to you, you are ready to begin. If you have identified even one small area you think might help you progress, you are ready to begin.

Remember, *brilliant execution is everything.* You did not read this book to just have something else to think about. You read it because you are a leader—and leaders act.

Now get to work!

If you want to reach out to discuss or gain further insight regarding anything contained in the book, please email me or my partner, Jason Thompson.

If you are willing to share your experiences, please email one of us. We'd love to hear your stories.

And if you are open to discussing how we might be able to assist you, by all means, email one of us. Our addresses are:

bill@axiesgroup.com
jason@axiesgroup.com

We look forward to hearing from you.

APPENDIX

Acknowledgments

BILL LEIDER

First and foremost, I want to thank Jason Thompson, my partner, friend, cofounder, and comanaging partner of Axíes Group. His collaborative efforts and input formed the core of our balanced organization model and helped shape the content of this book. His unique skills at making the strategic become tactical is an invaluable component in what makes the lessons of this book work.

Second, I want to thank Dr. Alfred Nicols, my economics professor when I was a student at UCLA. His one question final exam, *"What would it take to grow the world's wheat supply in a flower pot?"* planted the seed within me that slowly grew over the next twenty years of my life and eventually became a driving force in putting the legs of brilliant execution on the foundation of our balanced organization model. He's not with us anymore, but I hope he somehow receives my sincere thanks.

Thanks to the hundreds of leaders and thousands of followers I've encountered and worked with over the last forty-plus years for your contributions, conscious and unconscious, that enabled me to develop, fine-tune, test, and prove the effectiveness of the elements of balance and the actions needed to Master Your Balance.

My deepest thanks to some people whose contributions came over years of interaction and proved so valuable in shaping my work and putting it together in this book. Jeff Turner, a former client, partner, colleague, and friend. Our continuous conversations particularly influenced the shaping of how and how crucial values and values-driven leadership are in developing, leading, and growing exceptional organizations. Eric Openshaw, who began as my client and became my best and closest friend. His continuous rise throughout his career culminated in his becoming the vice chairman of Deloitte. Tragically, he passed away on July 20, 2015, from a sudden onslaught of glioblastoma. He taught me the art of having productive conversations with people of divergent points of view and making everyone stronger in the process. He is with me every day. Dr. Amir Vokshoor, a renowned neurosurgeon and the founder and CEO of INI (Institute of Neuro Innovation), where I am honored to serve as the vice president of the governing board. Our conversations and explorations have led to the inclusion of various aspects of neuroscience to guide the organic interactions of the elements of balance and serve to strengthen the quality of leadership and the performance of organizations. My daughter, Janet, whose critical reading of the manuscript provided invaluable guidance and clarity to what would otherwise have been a very messy collection of interesting stuff.

And finally, to my incredible, loving, caring, supportive, and beautiful wife, Arlene. Her constant, unwavering support and guidance was beyond inspirational. She is my rock. Without her, none of this would have come to be. Honey, thank you. I love you.

JASON THOMPSON

I owe a debt of gratitude to everyone who has taught me and worked with me over the years—professors, clients, friends and family. Your insight, support and perspective continue to influence me today. They are too numerous to mention; therefore, I will limit specific acknowledgments to a few key individuals whose contributions and unwavering support have enabled our work at Axíes Group to take shape.

Robert Thompson, my father, who instilled in me a strong work ethic at a young age. He often reminded me, "It's not worth doing if it's not done right."

John Estafanous, CEO at RallyBright, strategic partner to Axíes Group, and friend. Your collaboration, inspiration, and ongoing support have been instrumental.

Bill Leider, my friend, cofounder and comanaging partner of Axíes Group. Your friendship, rich experience and wealth of knowledge have been invaluable in creating the Axíes Balanced Organization model. This manuscript would not have been possible without your unique ability to powerfully share the transformational effects our clients have experienced leveraging the six elements of balance.

To my five beautiful daughters—Danielle, Madeline, Sadie, Lilli, and Janie—thank you for always being so supportive, encouraging and loving. I wouldn't be who I am today without you. I love you.

I wouldn't be where I am today without the unwavering support and love of my best friend, and beautiful wife. You inspire me on a daily basis with your kindness, intellect and drive to be better. Dixie, thank you. I love you.

ABOUT THE AUTHORS

Bill Leider is a seasoned, highly respected executive leader, advisor, and consultant. He is the managing partner of Axíes Group, a consulting company. He works with growth-minded leaders and organizations that want to propel their performance from acceptable to exceptional. They are companies that understand the value of, and invest in, enhancing their leadership skills. They embrace adaptability and resiliency because we live in a world where yesterday's achievements are not necessarily a roadmap to tomorrow's success. And Axíes Group is known for helping companies set and achieve unimagined goals.

Axíes Group has also developed a low-cost/high ROI balance assessment instrument designed to show leaders and their teams how their current performance compares to the performance of highly functional, successful teams across a broad spectrum of businesses and industries. This assessment enables leaders to see where they are in relationship to where they need to go to cross the bridge between acceptable and exceptional. It is an invaluable tool from which to develop the right strategies and better enable companies to brilliantly execute those strategies.

Bill also serves as the vice president of the governing board of INI (Institute of Neuro Innovation), a neuroscience research organization involved in improving brain health. Due to his involvement, he and Axíes Group have applied neuroscience findings to further strengthen leadership skills, behaviors, and results.

Bill is a regular guest lecturer in the Sol Price School of Public Policy at USC, where he lectures in leadership using the balanced organization model in a class in counterterrorism as a required part of the master's degree program.

Bill's first book, *Brand Delusions*, looks at brands through a holistic lens based on the definition of a brand as a widely held set of beliefs and expectations about what you deliver and how you deliver it, validated by your customers' experiences.

On the personal side, Bill and his wife Arlene pursue their interests in discovering new and delicious foods that are rich in healthy ingredients and don't contain refined sugar, gluten, or dairy. (Sounds crazy, right?) Arlene has an amazing talent for creating those kinds of dishes, and Bill is her avid taste-testing pilot. They are also involved in meditation and diaphragmatic breathing routines. It makes for a more enjoyable, less stressful, and fulfilling life. And their two dogs have become calmer in the process. Go figure.

Jason Thompson is the Managing Partner at Axíes Group. He provides a unique and powerful perspective drawn from thirty years' experience as both a corporate executive and a consultant. He has advised numerous companies in the areas of strategy, and execution from Fortune 500, mid-market and start-ups across many industries throughout the US.

Jason chairs a CEO peer advisory board, as well as mentoring CEOs from high growth companies.

He currently has the privilege of serving as Board President for Your Community Connection (YCC) Family Crisis Center in Ogden, Utah.

Jason and his wife Dixie have raised five beautiful and multi-talented daughters. They enjoy spending time together as a family creating fun memories; whether they're playing games, traveling, playing sports, or just hanging out.

Made in the USA
Las Vegas, NV
29 July 2021